THE CHRISTIAN MAN

The Christian Man

JIM SMITH

A Falcon Book

KINGSWAY PUBLICATIONS
EASTBOURNE

First published 1986

ISBN 0 86065 379 X

Falcon Books
are published by Kingsway Publications
in conjunction with the Church Pastoral Aid Society, an Anglican evangelical society committed to helping local churches in mission and growth.
CPAS Mission at Home, Falcon Court,
32 Fleet Street, London EC4Y 1DB.

Cover photo: Mick Rock, Cephas Picture Library

Printed in Great Britain for
KINGSWAY PUBLICATIONS LTD
Lottbridge Drove, Eastbourne, E. Sussex BN23 6NT by
Cox & Wyman Ltd, Reading.
Typeset by Nuprint Services Ltd, Harpenden, Herts AL5 4SE.

I dedicate this book
to the memory of my son Philip.
His three hours of life have taught me
so much about the pain and the privilege
of being a man in the
service of Christ.

Contents

INTRODUCTION

What Is a Christian Man Anyway?

It's two o'clock on a bitterly cold English Sunday afternoon, and instead of relaxing in a warm armchair, I'm standing outside a large football stadium. Christmas is very near, and the club want me to lead the crowd in some carol singing before the big match. This is quite an undertaking as twenty thousand people are expected. However, as an evangelist I'm excited about having the chance to speak to thousands of people—mostly men—who don't usually darken the doors of a church, unless they're carried in dead!

By 2.20 p.m. the ground is filling up, and I'm given the signal to start. Walking down the players' tunnel, and glimpsing the green grass ahead of me, I begin to feel really afraid, but all my fears disappear as soon as I get started. The choir and orchestra are very good, the crowd give me a fair hearing and I really enjoy myself, although after forty minutes I'm ready to stop and hand over to the professional footballers for the remaining ninety minutes. On my way home, I find myself wondering what the crowd made of it all. After all, they had paid to see a match, not to listen to me.

As I learnt sometime later, reactions on the terraces

had been very mixed. Some men had been singing, but others had taken the opportunity to go for a pre-match drink. Some were quite abusive, and in one corner of the stand, a group of men were making their feelings known. 'Who do you think you are,' they were shouting, 'coming here with all that religious rubbish? If we'd wanted to hear all that, we'd have gone to church.'

But one member of this group wasn't shouting. He had recently given control of his life to Jesus Christ at an evangelistic meeting in this very stadium, and he wanted to listen to what was being said. Eventually he could stand it no longer and he turned and shouted, 'Why don't you shut up and listen. You just don't know what you're missing.' It was hard to know who was the most shocked—the group doing the heckling, or the man for what he had said. Anyway it had the desired effect, and the heckling stopped.

Something had obviously happened to this man in the six months that he had been a Christian to give him the courage to make a public stand for Christ in a very public and hostile place. The Bible describes the change in this way:

> Don't let the world squeeze you into its mould, but let God remould your minds from within, so that you may prove in practice that the plan of God for you is good, and meets all his demands, and moves towards the goal of true maturity (Romans 12:2, J. B. Phillips).

A Christian man is a man who is fully surrendered to Jesus Christ. He is willing to let Christ remould that life from the inside. This process can be painful, slow and difficult, but it is ultimately very rewarding, making us men who can be fully used by Christ. This is the hallmark of the true Christian man. Many are willing to let Christ enter their lives, but resist this remoulding process, either because they don't realize its necessity, or they are not willing to face the cost and the consequences. The result of this resistance is weak and insipid Christian men who are of little use in the task of reaching others for Christ, and who do nothing for the building of the fellowship of believers.

My football supporter had begun to experience the remoulding process, which is why he did what he did, and in this book I'm going to look more closely at how Christ changes us, and at what sort of men he expects us to be.

It hasn't been an easy book to write, because I've had to keep stopping to examine my own attitudes to my wife and family, to the world, to money and possessions, and to my friends. I hope this will encourage you as you read and think about what I have written. Your problems are my problems and I struggle with them just as you do. But I have found that by living more closely to what the Bible teaches and by allowing Jesus to have more room to work in my life, I'm a more satisfied and fulfilled person. This has made all the changes worth while in the long run.

I do hope that many women will read this book. I'm not writing about and for men in order to downgrade women in any way. The family of believers is made up of men and women, who together allow Christ to work through them. I hope that this book will help women to understand men better—the struggle of our lives, the competitive instinct, the need to hide our feelings and emotions, the need to appear strong and able. As a consequence I hope that women will be better able to support us as we try to become the men God intended us to be.

After speaking at one seminar, a woman came up to me and said, 'I never realized how hard it was for a man to follow Christ until today. Now I'm going to pray much harder for the men of my church.' I hope that many women will feel the same after reading this book.

But even more, I want many men to read this book. I believe that those men who are not Christians, but are interested in the faith, will have a unique chance to see what will be asked of them if and when they become Christians. I also believe that Christian men reading this book will have the opportunity to become more Christlike and more effective with their non-Christian friends.

We are facing a very important moment in the history of our faith. Perhaps the trend of a declining male Christian presence can now be reversed. But if this dream is going to become a reality, then many Christian men—myself included—are going to have to take a very serious look at themselves in the light of what Jesus wants of us and has already said to us in the Bible. It's going to be a revolutionary experience for many of us. Are you prepared to let it be a revolutionary experience in your life?

I

A Man and His Personal Needs

In personal matters, a Christian man has a very different approach to that of a non-Christian man—or should have! The basis for this difference isn't to be found in our biological make up, or in our human desires. We're all very much the same in this respect whether we are Christians or not. It isn't to be found in a list of rules and regulations, which Christians are supposed to obey while non-Christians can do as they like. The basis of the difference is that we have surrendered our lives to Jesus Christ. We have given up doing things our way and now we are letting him have his way in our lives. Our purpose and desire is to be like him in every way, and the Bible sums it up for us in one verse: 'More than anything else, however, we want to please [Jesus]' (2 Corinthians 5:9).

A MAN AND HIS SEXUAL NEEDS

Let's not beat about the bush. Our sexual drives, emotions, feelings and needs are very high on our agendas. They have a major influence on what we do and say, so let's start with a look at the situation as it is, and then at some of the Christian options open to us.

Our sexual drives are a very positive attribute to our personal lives. People are quick to accuse Christians of being prudish and narrow over sexual matters, but actually nothing should be further from the truth. The Bible quite clearly states that sex and sexual attraction are part and parcel of God's plan for his creation. After all, he was the One who wrote the first manual on personal relationships, and he made his position clear on page one:

> So God created man in his own image, in the image of God he created him; male and female he created them. God blessed them and said to them, 'Be fruitful and increase in number; fill the earth and subdue it' (Genesis 1:27–28, NIV).

We seem to have managed to follow these instructions with very little problem, and have had a lot of fun doing so!

The problems have come because of what we have done with our basic and healthy sexual desires. Down the ages we've managed to mess the whole thing up. In our generation there's an erotic explosion bursting through society, and it's sweeping all before it. Fuelled by television, advertising and pornography, and flourishing in a promiscuous atmosphere, it is distorting our God-given drives and leading us into all kinds of excess. Our sexual balance is upset and we begin to believe that morals are what we make them. Our attitudes are shaped by immorality and we treat women very badly. If we can't watch them half naked on the television, or ogle them in the street, then we paw over them through pornography, or lust after them in secret, doing with our minds or in our fantasies what we would do for real if only we had the opportunity or the courage.

Most men have to find some outlet for their physical desire. Some turn to sport or work, and many to a deep and loving relationship with a wife—although even this can be spoilt by erotic fantasy. Some turn elsewhere for release—to masturbation stimulated by pornographic books or videos; some to deviations such as homosexuality, erotic parties, casual sexual relationships. Some turn to deviation within their marriages, doing things to and with their wives that others have suggested will bring heightened sexual experience.

Some become aggressive and violent towards women. Sexual harassment and rape are more common than official statistics reveal. The media report them in detail, because people want to read about them. Yet rape is a violent crime which devastates and ruins the life of the person against whom it is committed.

The Bible doesn't hide the dark side of the masculine nature from us. King David of Israel took another man's wife, had intercourse with her, and then arranged the murder of the husband when he found out that the woman had become pregnant. All this because he could not control his sexual reaction to a chance sighting of this woman bathing. David's son Amnon was no better than his father. He desired to have intercourse with his own sister, and through trickery contrived to rape her violently, causing her personal ruin and ultimately his own murder at the hands of one of his brothers.

These are ugly pictures and they should help us

become more aware of the difficult side to our God-given sexual instincts and desires. Writing this book has helped me become aware of my own attitudes and behaviour. I've come to realize that it's easy to live with the distortions without realizing what they are doing to me as a man, and to the women around me. As I've asked myself the hard questions I've been disturbed by what I have found within myself. What might you find if you examined your attitudes openly and honestly? For example:

* What stimulates your sexual desires?
* Are these stimuli right and healthy or not?
* What do you read and watch?
* Do you have sexual fantasies about certain women?
* Do these fantasies help you in your relationships with women, at work or in leisure time? Do they help you in your marriage?
* Do you find things in yourself that are disturbing?

The situation is made more confusing for men when we fail to appreciate that men and women experience sexual desire and arousal in very different ways. Generally speaking, a woman is more aroused by the character of a man, by the nature of her surroundings, by gentleness and consideration. A man is very physical—he wants to touch and see. He wants to make love with the light on, but she wants to be loved in the dark. He doesn't care about who's next door, but she is worried that the children might come in. He's in a hurry when roused—she isn't. He can't wait—she can. Her physical urge is initially nowhere near as strong as his, and abstinence is an easier option for her. For man, abstinence is a very tough option. The physical need for release is intense, and to go without is a daunting challenge.

Women don't always understand the masculine approach to sex—they tend to see men through their own eyes, and this can cause problems for us. Women often don't realize that the sight of a female body, walking, resting, swimming or dancing can trigger our desires. Mistakes can then so easily happen when we misunderstand a normal gesture for a 'come on' signal. Many a man is still puzzling over why he has had his face slapped when he thought he was moving forward with the woman's agreement. It's mostly due to this very different attitude to things sexual.

I believe that women are generally very naïve about the true nature of men's sexual instincts and desires, and are quite often amazed when men disclose these inner needs and tensions. I remember trying to explain the masculine approach to sexuality to a married woman, and no matter what I said, she didn't believe me. So in desperation I said, 'Would you mind pulling your skirt over your petticoat while we're talking. I'm finding it difficult to concentrate.' This helped her to understand a little more clearly, but it took a very open statement to get there. I remember too on one occasion a young woman coming to speak to me after a meeting. Her problem was that men wouldn't leave her alone, and she wanted to know why this was so. She was wearing a see-through blouse at the time and a very short skirt. She may have found it difficult to understand why men couldn't leave her alone, but I understood very quickly indeed!

Jesus was very clear on issues like this, and on the

style of sexual behaviour he expected of us, when he said:

> You have heard that it was said, 'Do not commit adultery.' But now I tell you: anyone who looks at a woman and wants to possess her is guilty of committing adultery with her in his heart (Matthew 5:27).

This verse comes very close to the heart of our problem as men. We're not all animals lusting after any and every woman, we want to control our sexual desires and to use them as God intended, we want to respect women as people, not as objects of sexual desire, but it's a struggle for us. The other day I was walking in the park with my children when I came across an interesting piece of graffiti painted on the side of the slide. It said quite simply: 'Girls—for a good time ring Steve on 91 1234.' I bet Steve didn't get many phone calls! He obviously didn't understand much about women. But every man reading that piece of graffiti understood everything about Steve!

Why bother to change anyway?—a Christian answer

If there are problems with our sexual attitudes as men—and I feel sure that there are—why should we bother to change them? After all, most of our problems are fairly harmless, aren't they? Surely looking at the girls on the beach doesn't do anyone any harm.

It is this kind of thinking that creates the problems for most of us. We're not likely to rape a woman, or commit an indecent assault, and women are safe with us. But it's in our minds that we lose the battle and many will tell us that it's a battle that doesn't need to be fought at all. The other day I went with a friend to buy a newspaper. After some deliberation, he chose the one with the nude woman on page three. Sensing my attitude, he said, 'I just like a little titillation, Jim. There's nothing wrong with that is there?' The non-Christian man would see nothing wrong with this attitude. He can make up his own moral standards and adjust his attitudes as he goes along.

But for the man who is surrendered to Jesus Christ, there's everything wrong with this kind of attitude. The things we think in our minds, see with our eyes and long for in our hearts—this is our battlefield. Do you ever find yourself looking at a woman in a desiring way, almost without knowing it? Do sexual fantasies invade your dreams? Do you watch things on TV that you know will have sexual overtones? This is the battlefield for the Christian and we all face this kind of pressure all the time. And worse, as we have seen, the Lord regards these inner feelings in just the same light as indecent assault, rape, adultery and the like (Matthew 5:27).

The Christian man wants to bring his thinking and actions into line with those of the Lord however hard this may be—it really is our aim to please him. What's more, we want our sexual drives and desires to be creative—as God intended them to be—part of the reflection of his glory in us. What reasons can Christ offer us for making the changes that he desires? Here are a few of the reasons, and I hope that each one will give some ideas for discussion, thought and prayer:

1. A Christian man knows that there are wrong attitudes buried in his sexual desires. He knows that he needs cleansing, release and a new pattern of

behaviour. Christ came for this very purpose. If a man has given himself to Christ, he has already recognized these facts. What better reason can there be for letting them influence his life? As you reflect on these things, consider these verses and their importance, for: 'When anyone is joined to Christ, he is a new being; the old is gone, the new has come' (2 Corinthians 5:17). Also:

> If we say that we have no sin, we deceive ourselves, and there is no truth in us. But if we confess our sins to God, he will keep his promise and do what is right: he will forgive us our sins and purify us from all our wrongdoing (1 John 1:8–9).

2. A Christian man knows that to resist the changes that God desires offends God, denies him his full blessing, and prevents him becoming the man God intended him to be. God has a clear goal for all his servants: 'We shall become mature people, reaching to the very height of Christ's full stature' (Ephesians 4:13).

We will never be able to reach this goal while some of our attitudes remain unchanged and untouched by him. Let's be quite clear on this—God isn't waiting for us to be perfect before we can be mature. If that were the case we would wait for ever. Nor is he for ever condemning us every time we make a mistake—he's very understanding and forgiving. But the intention of our hearts must be for change in our attitudes, even though it takes a lifetime to achieve. Is the intention of your heart to change? If it isn't, then you're in for trouble, and all of your own making: 'If I had ignored my sins, the Lord would not have listened to me' (Psalm 66:18).

3. A Christian man knows that he is part of the family of God. The family is made up of men and women, who in their joint and different ways serve God and the world. To allow unchanged sexual attitudes to affect our relationship with the female part of God's family degrades women and offends God. In some ways the battle is even hotter inside the family of God than it is outside. Inside the family we encourage relationships between men and women—young women and older men, married men and other men's wives, married women and single men—as part of our proclamation of the togetherness of the family and our unity in Christ. Therefore we need to be more sure than ever that our inner attitudes are right. Are yours?

4. Wrong sexual attitudes can spoil our relationships with our wives. They can turn the marvel of marital sex into something second rate as we search after some fantasy. Are you prepared to allow this sort of thing to spoil your marriage? There's also our responsibility to our children. They will take in our attitudes, or at least set their standards by what they see or don't see in us. Do you want their marriages to become spoilt one day because of your attitude?

On the positive side

Change is hard, but there are positive and rewarding reasons for it—the Christian life is a very positive and rewarding experience. Here are some of the positive aspects for your encouragement:

1. Change brings great joy to the Lord. He delights to see us changing into his likeness. All the filth, shame and pain that he endured on the cross was for this very purpose: 'Christ himself carried our sins in his body to

the cross, so that we might die to sin, and live for righteousness' (1 Peter 2:24).

Spend a few moments thanking God for the chance to change, for the power of the Holy Spirit who brings change, and for Jesus, who by his death has made all change possible. Perhaps there is a particular thing that is worrying you at the moment. Maybe what you have read has brought it to the surface. Bring it to Christ right now. Lay it at the foot of his cross, allow him to take it over, and be thankful.

2. Change really does bring release from past sins and failures, and the chance for a new beginning. As I've already mentioned, I've had to take a hard look at my attitudes and desires as I've prepared this book, and I've been led to make many changes. This has greatly deepened and enriched my marriage, given me a desire to want to help my four sons with their attitudes, and has been wholly creative and good. I've a long way to go, but the journey so far has been well worth it.

3. Change brings us more into line with the Bible. Not only does this bring us more into line with God's plan for our lives, but it also gives us strong foundations on which to build our moral standards in the face of an increasingly immoral and uncertain world.

> So then, anyone who hears these words of mine and obeys them is like a wise man who built his house on rock. The rain poured down, the rivers overflowed, and the wind blew hard against that house. But it did not fall, because it was built on rock (Matthew 7:24–25).

How do I change—what's expected?

This book is a 'sharing' book. By this I mean we're looking at shared joys and difficulties and trying to discover what Christ is expecting of us. It isn't a book of 'do's' and 'don'ts'. Please bear this in mind as you come across sections where practical advice is offered. These practical suggestions are only included as a guide—and if they don't seem relevant to your situation, or you can think of better practical ideas, do pass them over.

Here are some suggestions that might prove useful as you try to bring things under the rule of Jesus:

Think positive!

Our sexual 'personality' is not sinful, even though we may have messed it up. God can make all things new and longs to do so for you and me. It may look like an uphill task, but God specializes in uphill tasks. Jesus said: 'What is impossible for man is possible for God' (Luke 18:27). Are you thinking positive and believing that changes can occur?

Spend more time with Jesus

Rules and regulations can help us as a guide, but the best way to be more like Jesus is to spend more time in his presence. If you find it difficult to set aside more time, then why not invite him specifically into some of the 'spare' times of your day? Most of us have some 'slack' moment in the day—perhaps for a bath or tea-break—that we could use to spend time with Jesus. It's a question of finding it.

Ask for understanding

Sometimes it's hard to know in what ways we should be changing, or exactly what God wants us to do. Often we turn to books or friends for advice instead of turning to God. He has the advantage of knowing us intimately, and he has said: 'If any of you lacks wisdom, he should pray to God, who will give it to him' (James 1:5). Sometimes we hesitate to do this because we misunderstand the nature of God. He isn't a person who stands outside of our situation, waiting until we have got it right. On the contrary, he wants to get involved with us, helping us to find the right way forward. It's almost as if he says to us: 'Come on, let's work this out together.' Are you making the most of God's wisdom?

The feminine approach

Women approach sex and sexual matters in a very different way from men. My marriage has been strengthened as I've assimilated this fact and have tried to see things through my wife's eyes. I believe that many men would also find their eyes opened if they followed a similar approach. I went to the library and found books by and about women in the sociology section. Specifically Christian writers have also tackled this subject and local Christian bookshops can help here.

Your wife

Your wife can be of the greatest help to you. It takes courage on both sides—for you to share your inner self, and for her to listen and understand a man's world—but given the commitment, there's no greater comfort, friend and advisor than your wife. Mary and I have found that sharing these things takes time, as we each reflect on what we're sharing together, and our experience would suggest that taking it steady is the best way. Perhaps many of you are already sharing these things with your wife. If so, then you've cause for great rejoicing. If you're not, is this the time to make a start?

A friend

If you're not married then it's a great help to have a friend with whom you can share these things. Even if you are married, it helps to have someone—probably a man—with whom you can share. I have such a friend and I have found it of the greatest benefit. We've been friends for a long time, but it's only recently that we've begun to share these matters. Have you got such a friend?

Avoiding action

There's nothing wrong with being tempted. A man once said to me: 'Jim, I keep having these awful dreams where I'm doing terrible things with women. How can I be a Christian when this is happening to me?' I asked him whether he wanted or enjoyed the dreams, and he gave me an emphatic 'No!', so I said: 'Then let's give all the dreams to the Lord, and you can stop worrying. There's nothing wrong with being tempted. The problem only comes when we give in to temptation.'

Perhaps I should take my own advice more, because last week I got in late from work and turned on the television to find that I was watching a French film with subtitles. I knew that this was a pornographic film, but to my shame continued watching.

I could have avoided this situation by turning off the TV as soon as I knew what was on. Quite a lot of things are avoidable. For example:

* Control your TV switch, the buying of papers, magazines, etc. (I've stopped subscribing to one of the main video magazines because I found adverts for pornography in the back. Not good for me, or for my boys.)

* Control what passes through your ears. What men talk about sometimes can be difficult to cope with, but we can always move out of earshot, or perhaps we have to speak out ourselves.

* Control your marriage. What goes on between a man and his wife is not always as pure and wholesome as it should be. Your marriage is the one main area over which you have some control. Are there things that you are doing with your wife which would make you ashamed if the Lord came and found you doing them? Are you setting a good example for your children? Why not ask them, if they are old enough?

* Control your relationships. We must be aware of ourselves in all our relationships with women, but occasionally a particular woman can trigger our fantasies. These relationships need particularly careful handling—perhaps we need to make the relationship a little more formal, as a guard against disaster.

'Releasing' experience

Most of us get overheated occasionally. How do we find release? Married men can spend time with their wives, although this isn't always possible at the crucial moment. It's important for each of us to learn how we can release our tensions. For example:

* A distraction to break the pattern of thought.
* Sports: squash, golf, a walk.
* A hobby.
* Concentrate on the work in hand.
* Shower and/or sleep.

Coming to terms with our need for release is in itself a release. Do you have a releasing method?

Resist

Christian men have got to have iron in their soul. It is a battle sometimes to resist and we need to see it as such. When thoughts get hold of us, we must not say: 'Oh no, not that again!' but follow the Bible's advice: 'Take every thought captive and make it obey Christ' (2 Corinthians 10:5).

Do you capture your unwelcome thoughts and give them to Christ in prayer? We need to be determined, recognizing that we're up against a determined foe who has to be fought in the power of Christ. Are you taking your stand for God's morality, inside of your own mind in your home, place of work, or leisure?

It's too late for me now

Perhaps some men reading this book have already succumbed to some or many of the temptations that surround us all. Maybe some have given in to pre-marital or extra-marital sex, to fantasy or deviation, to the lure of pornography, to adultery or rape. Is it too late to change? The Bible teaches us that we follow a loving, understanding and forgiving God. To confess and ask to begin again is very costly, but it's a genuine option. These verses have always encouraged me:

> If we live in the light...the blood of Jesus, his Son, purifies us from every sin. If we say that we have no sin, we deceive ourselves, and there is no truth in us. But if we confess our sins to God, he will keep his promise and do what is right: he will forgive us our sins and purify us from all our wrongdoing. If we say that we have not sinned, we make God out to be a liar, and his word is not in us (1 John 1:7–10).

Perhaps for some it might be good to spend a little time alone now, thinking about God's forgiving nature and reading these verses through. Ask him to show you the way forward for a new beginning and ask him to find you a friend. Here is a brief prayer:

> Heavenly Father, I'm sorry for the
> sins of my eyes.
> Heavenly Father, I'm sorry for the
> sins of my mind.
> Heavenly Father, I'm sorry for the
> sins of my body.
> Heavenly Father, I'm sorry for any
> woman I have hurt, physically or in
> my mind.
> You said that the blood of Jesus will
> cleanse me.
> Please do that now.

A MAN AND HIS MASCULINITY

At first glance, it may seem strange to be considering this subject—surely we all know what a man is, don't we? Biologically of course we do, but it isn't our biological function that is in question. What is in question is the position of a man in a society that has abandoned the Bible as its guide and is therefore forced to make up its own rules. This leads inevitably to much confusion about the masculine role, both in this country and further afield. There are a number of factors which are causing this confusion and it is important to understand them, because against their background we will be able to judge more clearly what the Christian position has to offer us.

A man in marriage

A large change has come over society's attitude to marriage in recent years. One sociologist has described the change in this way: 'Segregated conjugal roles are changing to become joint conjugal roles' (Nobbs, Hine and Fleming). In other words, the distinctive contribution of the male and the female to the marriage relationship is being blurred. Roles are being mixed, even interchanged, as seems right to those involved. The Bible shows us that this blurring is not the will of God. He has clearly defined the roles as loving submission and committed love: 'Wives, submit to your husbands as to the Lord. For a husband has authority over his wife just as Christ has authority over the church' (Ephesians 5:22). And: 'Husbands, love your wives just as Christ loved the church and gave his life for it' (Ephesians 5:25).

Society seems content with joint conjugal roles, and in general ignores these biblical principles. But the price to be paid for this disregard is a weakening of the distinctive masculine role. This also has consequences for women, because if the man cannot be what God intended him to be in the marriage then neither can the woman, because the balance will not be right.

A man and his work

Times of high unemployment add much confusion to our understanding of our masculinity. Most of us have been taught from our mother's knee that we will and must get a job. Having a job has been seen as a sign of masculinity and people who fail to get and hold down a job have been looked upon as malingerers or worse.

It's very hard for men to live with these expectations when so many—and not the malingering type—cannot find work. It makes them feel impotent, unsure of themselves and their place in the order of things. In an increasing number of homes, the wife has been forced into the bread-winning role to support the family. This may provide an income, but it raises many problems for the unemployed man.

The rise of feminism

The rise of feminism may have done much for women in the twentieth century, but at the same time it has been a significant factor in the confusion which surrounds the role of man today. This movement has affected, and is still affecting, our wives, daughters, sisters, mothers, girlfriends and colleagues, and it's time we faced up to this fact and its implications for us.

I believe that this female liberation movement has not just brought confusion to men, but has also confused the female position as well.

I am not an expert on feminism, nor am I against all its aims and objectives. But a look at its basic position reveals the inherent danger in the movement to the biblical understanding of the place of men and women.

What is 'feminism'?

Feminism is not a bunch of bra-burning fanatics! It is a reaction against much of the bondage endured by women in past generations, and there was much that needed changing. Under the general title of feminism, women have banded together to get a better deal from society for women in general and much that is good has been achieved. Perhaps if men had been more prominent in the move to set women free from some of the medieval shackles that held them, then we wouldn't have quite so much of a problem today. Only the most arrogant and thoughtless of men would want to return to the ways of the past.

However, feminism has gone beyond liberation into wanting to create a new order of things. Here is the feminists' basic position as I understand it today:

1. There is no basic distinction between man and woman apart from the biological one.
2. All other differences are the result of social, cultural, or educational conditioning, designed by the male group to ensure their continued domination.
3. Women have the right to total equality with men. This is the path of liberation and freedom.
4. Women have the right not only to equality but to dominance over men, if the opportunity arises.

I believe these principles, now a part of society's

everyday thinking, are very damaging—to women as well as to men. Ordinary women are finding their potential for a full life being restricted. The Bible gives us a very beautiful picture of a faithful wife and mother (Proverbs 31), yet this position is under great threat today. A girl is not given the freedom to select this option for herself at school. She must have a career, or training for a job. Even if she doesn't want to have a job, the choice of marriage and motherhood as a 'career' isn't given to her. For an increasing number of women, a baby is just a temporary halt in the business of earning money, or being fulfilled in a career. The increase in baby-minders is making this possible, but is this what God intended? Feminists would presumably see this as liberation, but from God's point of view it could be seen as deterioration. For all the so called freedom of female liberation, society has deteriorated and is still doing so. Could it be that we have stepped outside of God's plan for the sexes?

The Bible also gives clear guidelines about the place of a woman in marriage (Ephesians 5:22–23)—she is to be submissive to her husband, for this is God's intention and purpose. Yet any woman who wants to live by this God-given standard comes under pressure from her friends and from the expectation of a society that sees a woman's place differently. The feminists would see submission as 'bondage', or at best old-fashioned. Yet this is what God intended and the woman who lives by this rule gives her husband the most room to fulfil his unique position in marriage. When he's doing that, then she too will grow in potential.

Recently, a Christian woman shared her thoughts with me on this subject, and they are my views too, because I believe they point the path to true liberation. She said: 'I'm getting closer to Jesus since I started coming to church. Now I'm concerned about my husband. I've always been an aggressive sort of person, but I've decided to let him be the head of the household. It isn't that I let him keep me under his thumb, but I let him lead. It's been tremendous! I never would have believed the difference it could make. It's taken the pressure off me and he's not even a Christian—yet! But he's softening and I hope that he will see the difference Christ is making to my life.'

So without reference to God, I believe that it is very difficult to understand exactly what a man is meant to be and to do today. Faced with this confusion many men just shrug their shoulders and say: 'Why not let things be? If women want a bigger say, if they want to blurr the marriage roles, if they want to be bread winners, why not let them get on with it?'

Most of us can understand this feeling and the women's liberation movement would applaud it as non-chauvinistic. But God has another word for it—disobedience. For he designed a unique position for a man, and when we occupy it, not only are we fulfilled to the utmost, but women are then truly liberated to be who God intended them to be. To reject this unique position, either through principle or ignorance, must be an offence to him.

Let's consider God's plan for man now and some of the implications for us. Most of the ideas are developed more fully elsewhere in this book. What is uniquely masculine about many of them is the way we view them and apply them to our lives. But looking at them is not enough. We must be prepared to live by the plan as well if we want to claim the title 'Christian man'.

God's plan for masculinity

Men are chosen by God

Many men have got so disillusioned or hardened, that they have lost sight of one of God's great truths. Jesus summed it up when he said to his disciples: 'You did not choose me; I chose you' (John 15:16). God is a choosing God and he chooses to use men, as well as women, in his plan and purpose. This is God's positive affirmation of our usefulness to him as men, to be set against all the confusion of our society. God, knowing us from the inside, and understanding us completely, values us so much as men that he chooses to use us.

God chooses and uses women as well, knowing their distinctive characteristics and potential. I'm not trying to put women down, but rather I'm trying to encourage men to believe what women have never doubted—God has a unique place for each of us. We're special, important and precious to him. Our women never seemed to have doubted it. Now it's time for the men to move alongside them and believe this as well.

It's important to realize at the outset that our unique masculine role is not ours by right. We can't demand to be given our position under God. Our position is a free gift to us from God, given by him, guaranteed by him and shaped by him. Our responsibility under him is to work out what this means in practice in our daily lives and relationships. This should leave no room for pride or arrogance. After all, what have we got to be proud or arrogant about? Our position is not of our own choosing, but it is a gift from God. This humility in leadership should guarantee the security of our women, not undermine it. When men humbly accept

God's gift, women have the potential to be more free than a million years of feminism could ever make them.

Pause right now to thank God for the privilege of being a man in his service. Ask him to make you more aware of the potential that you have to work for him.

Chosen for a purpose

To sum up God's purpose in a few pages is quite a tall order! Here are some indications and perhaps they will serve as the starting point for discussion. Some of what I'm saying here will apply to women as well. I can only repeat that I'm not in any way trying to denigrate the position of women. Rather I'm trying to help men see what God has in his heart for us, so that we, like so many Christian women, can achieve our potential.

(a) Chosen for headship of wife and family. Here are two passages from the Bible on this matter which need to be looked at together. Do they describe your attitude to your wife?

> For the husband is the head of the wife as Christ is the head of the church (Ephesians 5:23, NIV). Husbands, be considerate as you live with your wives, and treat them with respect as the weaker partner, and as heirs with you of the gracious gift of life (1 Peter 3:7, NIV).

(b) Chosen for leadership of the body of Christ. For far too long much of the work in our churches and fellowships has been led by women. We don't have to look very far for the reason do we? Most men have abdicated their spiritual responsibilities in favour of their women. The task of instructing the children and leading much of

the work in the fellowship has fallen to the women. The men won't lead, so the women have had the job thrust on them. Men feel that they have lost their right or opportunity to lead and they won't come back and take it up. So a vicious circle is created and the women continue, while their daughters predominate in the youth fellowships with the strong opportunity of moving into leadership positions within the adult fellowship, following in the footsteps of their mothers.

I don't believe God intended it to be this way. Throughout the pages of the Bible, when he wanted a job that required positive leadership, he would turn to a man. We're ideally equipped to occupy a leadership role because we are initiators. We need the women right beside us of course, and when they are in that position they're truly able to fulfil themselves and so are we. The fault for the position we find ourselves in doesn't lie entirely with the men or the women. Until quite recently, many ministers and full-time elders showed little apparent concern for the lack of men in the church. The work of the church seemed structured in such a way as to avoid men: visiting in the day time, putting on meetings just after men got in from a hard day's work, clashing with family bedtimes and so on. Fortunately I really do believe that times are changing. There is a rising tide of concern for reaching men and much greater discussion and thought about how this might be achieved. Is this the case in your heart and in your fellowship? If not, why not?

(c) Chosen to serve. The rest of the verse from John 15 which we looked at earlier helps us to understand this part of our purpose: 'You did not choose me; I chose you and appointed you to go and bear much fruit, the kind of fruit that endures' (v.16).

God has chosen us for his service. We are his tools for him to use as he brings more and more people to know and love his Son. We are certainly not chosen so that we can sit in cosy fellowships, singing praise choruses and enjoying each other's company. God wants to use us—at home, in our place of work, unemployment, leisure or wherever we happen to be.

(d) Chosen to suffer. When St Paul was called to follow Christ (Acts 9), he was blinded by the experience, so Jesus sent a man named Ananias to heal this blindness. Look carefully at what Jesus says to Ananias:

> This man is my chosen instrument to carry my name before the Gentiles and their kings...I will show him how much he must suffer for my name (Acts 9:15–16, NIV).

Suffering, hurt and pain are a part of the Christian life, and a man must expect this if he wants to be a true follower of Christ. Are you prepared to pay whatever price is necessary in order to become the man God intended you to be?

(e) Chosen to share. Men are chosen to share the good news of Jesus with other men. It's time we stopped expecting the women to do this job and took it on ourselves. I believe that a man needs to hear about Christ from another man. We are able to give the gospel that masculine appeal so necessary to reach the hearts of non-believing men. This is our responsibility and privilege.

(f) Chosen to be changed. God expects to be allowed to change us so that we become more like Jesus. This is particularly painful to men because we are so proud, and so sure of ourselves. Yet we must be prepared to

let it happen. Changing is a very positive experience. St Paul describes it like this:

> All of us, then, reflect the glory of the Lord with uncovered faces; and that same glory, coming from the Lord, who is the Spirit, transforms us into his likeness in an ever greater degree of glory (2 Corinthians 3:18).

It's impossible to sum up the whole of God's purpose for a man. This is just a brief sketch to make our mouths water! How do you measure up? What other facets would you want to add? I believe that by trying to understand God's plan for man, and by making it part of our lives, men *and* women can grow together in the service of Christ and forward his work here on earth.

The question might be asked: 'OK, that's all very interesting, but why should I bother to become this sort of a man?'

It's the willingness to bother that marks the difference between the Christian and the non-Christian man. The non-Christian man has the freedom not to bother. He can let his wife 'get on with it'. He can be a chauvinist or not as he feels like it; he can oppress or dominate, and he can let his wife run the marriage, the family and the budget. He needn't bother with leadership or service. He hasn't got to worry about suffering for the name of Jesus, nor being changed from what he is to what he could become. The surrendered man cannot take up this position for a number of compelling reasons:

a) He knows that this kind of approach is not what God intends or wants.

b) He wants to be the man God intends and he

knows that consequently he must fit in with God's plan for a man.

c) He wants a woman to achieve her full potential and this won't happen if he isn't achieving his potential.

d) He wants other men to find Christ and this won't happen if the Christian man looks insipid and hopeless.

Some practical suggestions

In the end, it all comes down to the question of how much we want to be like Jesus. If we really want this with our whole hearts, then we'll let God get to work, changing our human masculinity into the shape and form that he intends, the shape and form that will most please him and best fit us to match what he intends for women. Here are some ideas that are worth considering as you think and discuss this process.

Truly surrendered

The obvious starting point for being a Christian man is to be truly surrendered to Jesus—in every part of our life. The idea of surrender comes hard to men, but unless we're prepared to fall at his feet and put our lives completely and unconditionally in his hands, we'll never be able to become like Jesus.

Why not examine your life quietly and see if there are any areas that are not surrendered to him. For example: language, use of money, style of life, marriage, job, family. Don't leave out the dark corners either—pride, jealousy, arrogance, etc. Perhaps you haven't surrendered to Christ at all yet, but are reading this to discover what the differences might be if you did. You'll find that the next chapter deals more fully with the matter of how we give control of our lives to Jesus for the first time.

Build on the Bible

We've looked at the Bible on a number of occasions already, and we're going to look at it much more as we go along. Has anything struck you as particularly relevant or important to your life? Perhaps that's an area that God wants to develop or change.

It's not always easy to understand just what it is that God expects of us. That's one reason why the Bible is so useful—it's a book full of men's lives, and the record of how God worked with them and through them. As we look at how God dealt with them, we'll get a better idea of how he might want to deal with us. Here are seven men whose lives it might be useful to read and think about. As you read about them, try to imagine how you would have reacted and what God is trying to teach.

* *Joshua* (Joshua 1–11)
* *Jeremiah* (Jeremiah 1, 12–13, 20, 26, 28, 32, 36–43)
* *David* (1 Samuel 16—2 Samuel 24)
* *Manoah* (Judges 13)
* *Paul* (Acts 9–28)
* *Peter* (Mark 1, 8, 14; Acts 1–10)
* *Jesus* (All of Mark's gospel, which can be read in an hour!)

Leading, hurting, serving

Here are a series of questions that you might like to ask yourself, or discuss with your friends, concerning these three issues. Not every question will be relevant to you, but perhaps one or two will strike relevant chords.

Do you take the lead in your marriage? How can you become the spiritual head without hurting your wife? Is God calling you to some position of leadership at work or at church? Have you considered the possibility? Do you already lead at home, work or church? If you do, then what kind of leader do others see you to be? For example, are you compassionate or aggressive? Approachable or insular? Infallible or human? Stern or warm?

How do you react when you're hurt in any way? Do you lash out in anger? Sulk? Do you ever get hurt because you love Christ and want to live his way? How can you share the pains and hurts of your wife and family, your friends and colleagues?

Do you want to be known as a servant of others? (See the example of Jesus in John 13.) How do you see yourself as a servant? Do you have a servant heart? For example, would you consider doing some menial task that would normally be done by your wife, or your kids, as a sign of your willingness to serve both them and Christ?

Stand firm

Once we have got—or are getting—a clearer grasp of what Christ wants for us as men, then it's essential that we stand firm in what we believe. We need to stand against the excesses of feminism on the one hand, and the excesses of male chauvinism on the other. At the same time we must resist the lures of the 'why bother' brigade in the middle. At home, work or rest, if others are to see the difference, and if our sons and grandsons are to get a biblical view of man, then we must stand firm for Christ's sake. We must be men for Christ and Christlike for men.

A MAN AND HIS WEAKNESS

What is the popular image of a man? We might all have slightly different ideas, but there's a hard core of common truth. A man is strong, confident and able, and very much in control of himself and his environment. A man is definite in what he believes, dominant, quick to take the lead, and has much latent aggression which can easily boil over. A man hides his feelings and his emotions and he's not expected to cry. In fact when he does, it gives cause for comment. On a recent television programme a doctor said: 'When a woman comes into my surgery and starts to cry, I obviously care, but it isn't that uncommon. When a man comes in and starts to cry, I sit up and take notice.' On the same programme a factory foreman said: 'When I see a woman crying in the factory, I don't take a lot of notice. When I see a man crying, I assume that he's having a nervous breakdown.'

The real truth is that we're all very good actors. We have feelings—as strong as those of women and as much in need of release—but because of the image, we're unable to release them. We're often weak and in need of comfort and strength. When my fourth son, Philip, died I was devastated inside, but I didn't know how to cope with the emotions. I so needed help, but because I was stuck with the masculine 'image', I couldn't ask for it, or find it. So I quietly fell apart, with no one able to help me.

Is what I'm saying true in your life? Do you know

the feeling of weakness? Do you know what it's like to want to share feelings and emotions and yet to be trapped by the image? Are any of your friends trapped by the image?

This unwillingness to face up to our weaknesses has serious consequences for us. It means that we come off very badly in the crises of life—most of which have heavy emotional overtones. In sickness, redundancy, bereavement, family problems, money problems, personality and relationship problems, divorce and long-term separation, or any other big crisis, we do not shine.

Nor do we shine when failures come our way, or our inadequacy is exposed. That's the real problem with a tough guy image. We don't show or share our hurts and so we're deprived of the human support and encouragement we all need.

At the root of it, we've made a fundamental mistake. We think that appearing tough, upright and strong is strength, whereas it is really weakness because it deprives us of the love and support we need. We can turn to drink, cigarettes, sport and holidays for temporary relief, but until we change our basic philosophy, we will never be strong.

The men of the Bible worked to a different philosophy. St Paul, the great preacher of the early years of Christianity, was often under great stress and he let it show. He said: 'When I am weak, then I am strong' (2 Corinthians 12:10).

He had discovered that God was able to use men who knew and accepted their weaknesses, and consequently he wasn't afraid to show them, or share them. Quite a different approach to that employed by so many men today of 'hide it and endure it'.

If you're feeling the weakness and loneliness of being a man, then this verse from St Paul is a great beacon of hope and strength. Why not think about it for a while before you read on?

A Christian point of view

The non-Christian world has very few genuine answers to living with weakness. There are always those who will lend a listening ear to us of course and offer some kind of help. But the truth is that we need help inside and no amount of suggestion or self-help can provide this inner help. There are plenty of folklore answers of course—'have another drink', 'pull yourself together', 'have a holiday' and many more. They should be treated with the contempt they deserve.

It's a fallacy to think that the Christian man will find it any easier to accept his weaknesses than a non-Christian man. We are struggling with the same problems, caught by the same image, living in the same world. In some ways it's harder for us, because we can't allow ourselves the luxury of accepting any of the world's self-help ideas. Neither can we fail to hear the gentle but persistent voice of Jesus.

We do have some resources to draw on within the love of God, but before we look at them, let's be clear about one thing—there's no magic wand to remove all our problems. If there were, I can assure you that I would have found it by now. As I've wept over my own inadequacy, grieved for my son, and regretted the latent aggression which has damaged so many of my relationships, I've wished for a short cut. But there isn't one, and now that the years have passed, I can see that I'm a better man for being made aware of my weakness by God. I still regret the mistakes of course, and I've done all I can to put them right. Some of them I now realize can never be undone. I've had to accept these truths about myself and as a consequence, I never hesitate now to ask others for help if I need it, and I so often do. I believe that I'm infinitely stronger now than I was when I was too proud to ask.

There are some tremendous encouragements to be found in the Bible. Whether you know Christ or not, I commend these encouragements to you man to man. If you know Christ already, you can claim these encouragements for yourself straightaway. If you don't know Christ, you might like to consider them and weigh them against 'have another drink', 'have a holiday', 'pull yourself together', and see which seems the most genuine and appealing.

God understands men from the inside

As we look at the sort of men God has employed in the past, it should encourage us greatly. Moses was a murderer, lacking in confidence and unwilling to serve, yet he became the man God chose to lead the people of Israel out of slavery in Egypt. He was the man that God chose to give the Ten Commandments to. Would you have chosen him?

David was a weak man when it came to family and morality. He committed adultery and murder, and failed to be the master of his own house, yet God chose him to be the greatest king Israel ever knew.

Peter was arrogant, cocksure and finally a traitor, denying Jesus in the courtyard of the high priest, yet God chose him to be the key man in the first few years of the new Christian church.

Paul was probably the worst of the lot—he was a bigot, a thug and a murderer. He was completely without compassion, dragging Christians from their homes, imprisoning them, forcing them to blaspheme, arranging beatings and punishments. Yet God chose him to be the greatest missionary the church has ever known.

These great men were weak men and God knew it, but that didn't stop him using them. Paul puts this into words for us when he says:

> God purposely chose what the world considers nonsense in order to shame the wise, and he chose what the world considers weak in order to shame the powerful (1 Corinthians 1:27).

God understands you and yet he still wants to use you. Why not spend a few moments now bringing your weaknesses to him and thanking him for using you despite yourself?

God loves us with an eternally strong love

God knows that it's a struggle for us coming to terms with his strength and our weakness. He knows how painful this is and he really cares about it. He loves us with a very strong and deep love. If you've ever been tempted to think that God doesn't understand your situation, or doesn't want to get involved in it, here are some verses to think about to help you understand God's commitment to you:

> Since the children, as he calls them, are people of flesh and blood, Jesus himself became like them and shared

their human nature. He did this so that through his death he might destroy the Devil, who has the power over death, and in this way set free those who were slaves all their lives because of their fear of death... This means that he had to become like his brothers in every way, in order to be their faithful and merciful High Priest in his service to God, so that the people's sins would be forgiven. And now he can help those who are tempted, because he himself was tempted and suffered (Hebrews 2:14–18).

He uses our failures

God doesn't just forgive failure and leave it at that, but he is able to turn failure to creative use. This is something that the world can never mimic and will never be able to understand, but this is God's way. Compare the story of Peter's failure (Mark 14:66–72) with the story of his new commission and task (John 21:15–19). Would you have given Peter another chance? Thank God that he does give us a second—and a third—and a fourth—and a thousandth chance. God's approach to failure is summed up in the Bible in this way: 'We know that in all things God works for good with those who love him, those whom he has called according to his purpose' (Romans 8:28).

Have you made some terrible mistake? God can turn it to good, if you'll let him.

God treats us as men, not as children

When we make mistakes, God forgives and heals, but sometimes we are left with the memory and even the consequences. God isn't a puppet master who pulls all the strings and leaves us to dance. Nor is he a big daddy who gives us sweets and says: 'There, there, it will soon be better.' That would reduce us to the status of children, and God needs men.

It has taken many years to receive God's healing for the loss of our son, and I'm grateful to him for all he has done in me, to help and heal. But Philip hasn't been restored to us. With God's help I've got to learn to live with this. Sometimes I've cried my heart out and asked all the normal 'why' questions. But although God loves me, he wouldn't treat me as a child, with the 'there, there' approach. I'm glad now that God did treat me as a man, and while he has helped me immeasurably, at the same time he has made my shoulders just that bit broader to live with the consequences. I've had to learn to be a man in his service.

There's just a trace of this same experience in John's gospel. After Jesus had come back to life, he gave Peter a new commission and a new job. But before doing so, he asked him three times: 'Peter, do you love me?' I wonder if the memory of his three denials came into Peter's mind? Jesus also asked: 'Peter, do you love me more than these others?' It was Peter's arrogant assertion, 'I will never leave you, even though all the rest do' (Mark 14:29), that was the cause of his undoing in the first place, and again I suspect that at this moment it came to his mind, and did many times in the future, yet he still became a great leader.

Consequences—are there any in your life due to your mistakes? Ask God to help you to start coming to terms with them right now. Perhaps you've been praying that God would take them all away, but is it possible that he wants them to stay, to help you become a man in his service?

Our feelings are safe with him

God can be trusted to share our feelings without either rejecting us, or revealing them to others. We can be as sad, as angry or as disturbed as we like with him—he can and will take it. In Psalm 51, David came honestly before God, sharing his feelings after he had committed adultery with Bathsheba. If God is prepared to listen to this sort of thing, then he's surely prepared to listen to anything I can tell him, however sad, bad or ugly. Why not treat him more as a trusted friend and start sharing your innermost feelings with him?

I had planned to finish this section with some practical suggestions about living with our weaknesses. But I know that I find it hard to accept advice in this area of my life, and in print it could prove even more difficult to accept. I have found that my close friends have been my greatest help. They already know what I am like, yet they remain my friends and they are prepared to listen to me, and help where they can. My closest friend is my wife, and as I've had the courage to tell her what I'm really like and how I feel, I have found her support of the highest value. Sharing our strengths is fairly easy, but it takes courage to share our weaknesses.

So far we have looked at three of our personal needs—sexuality, masculinity and weakness. But there is a fourth: the need to live at peace with ourselves and the world around us. Inner peace is a spiritual quality, not a physical one, and no amount of physical activity can generate it. But if a man can't make or buy inner peace, then how does he get hold of it?

2

A Man and His Spiritual Needs

A MAN AND HIS NEED FOR GOD

If a man wants to live at peace with himself, then he has got to get things right between himself and God. There is no way round this process because God is the controlling influence in the universe, and to try and live at peace without being right with him is impossible.

But how does a man get things right between himself and God? I've tried to answer this question basing my answer on six questions that I'm often asked by men while discussing the Christian faith. Christian men reading this section may find some useful discussion starters with their non-Christian friends at work, at home, or in some informal setting.

Question 1: Why do I need God anyway?

A spirit of powerlessness has found its way into the world in which we live. It's clearly seen internationally where politicians are assassinated, ordinary people are maimed and killed by terrorist outrages and millions live at the point of starvation. It's fairly safe to assume that most people, of whatever creed, race or colour, do not want to see this kind of thing happening, but we're powerless to stop it.

The powerlessness is also to be found locally in our towns, on our streets, in our families and in our lives. There is so much happening around us which we do not like or want—solvent abuse by the young, family breakdown, crime, violence and moral decay. We don't like it, but no matter what we do, we seem powerless to stop it.

This powerlessness has also found its way into the lives of many men, and shows itself in the questions that often come up during discussion about religion. Have you ever asked yourself any of these?

* Why is the world like it is today?
* Why is it that despite my best efforts I can't seem to make more of my life?
* Why is it that I can't find lasting satisfaction?
* What will happen if I stop being successful?
* Why has my life become so mundane and ordinary? What happened to all my dreams?
* Why is my life in such a muddle?
* Why do I do wrong when I want to do right?
* How will people react if I fail?
* Why am I afraid to die?

Why are we so powerless? Why are we so insecure? Why can't we find inner peace? We can begin to answer these questions when we recognize that we are spiritual people, not just physical ones. The real 'us' is a spiritual 'us', living inside a body, and it's this part which is of supreme importance because our spiritual personality will live for ever. Our consumer society, with its emphasis on the here and now, discourages us from spending time considering our spiritual needs. The world has no medicine to offer for the spiritual needs, hurts, sorrow, frustration and pain that so many feel today. There is nothing to stop the spirit of powerlessness from sweeping in and wrecking our lives, and that's precisely what has happened to so many. Has it happened to you?

The only place to turn for help is to the greatest spiritual force in the universe; to God, the Creator of all things.

Unfortunately for us, there has been a breakdown in our communication with God. One psalmist puts it like this:

> I am surrounded my many troubles—too many to count! My sins have caught up with me, and I can no longer see; they are more than the hairs of my head, and I have lost my courage (Psalm 40:12).

We have said, done and thought things that are wrong and the Bible calls these things 'sin'. God doesn't want us to sin, but we do, and we go on doing it. Have you ever tried to stop swearing, or thinking wrong things, for example? How long have you managed to last out? Our sins mark us off as rebels against God's will, so he's broken off communication with us. We left him no choice.

This has serious consequences, both for now and for ever. For now we are totally exposed to the powerless spirit. It has full freedom to wreck everything we had hoped for. It can spoil us, our children, our marriage, our home, our nation, our world. In the eternal context: 'For sin pays its wage—death' (Romans 6:23).

Eternally we are ruined by the spirit of powerlessness. It has driven us apart from God and we face eternity knowing that through our deliberate choice, we are separated from God for ever. Why do you need God? Only God can make sense of your life. Without him you haven't a hope of living at peace with yourself. The Bible describes the ultimate fate of life without God like this:

> So life came to mean nothing to me, because everything in it had brought me nothing but trouble. It had all been useless; I had been chasing the wind (Ecclesiastes 2:17).

Question 2: Does God want me?

This is the right question for a man to ask, especially when he begins to realize his true position before God. It's also the question I most enjoy answering, because it can be put in one lovely word—*yes*! God made his desire quite clear when he said: 'I have loved you with an everlasting love' (Jeremiah 31:3, NIV).

Despite everything, God longs to have us back at his side. To make this possible he sent his only Son, Jesus Christ, to offer us a new arrangement, a new deal, a new start, if we really want it. The Bible explains how this is possible.

Jesus offers the chance of peace with God

In the story of the paralysed man (Mark 2:2–12), Jesus was preaching in Capernaum, and he was so popular that the house he was speaking at was full to capacity. So when four men arrived, carrying their paralysed friend on a bed, they couldn't get in to see Jesus. But being resourceful men, they climbed up onto the roof, removed the covering of branches and lowered their friend down to Jesus, using ropes tied to a bed. The story continues: 'Seeing how much faith they had, Jesus said to the paralysed man, "My son, your sins are forgiven"' (v. 5).

In this story, Jesus clearly claimed to have the power to deal with sin, and he was prepared to back up that claim with a demonstration of his power as the story continues:

> 'I will prove to you, then, that the Son of Man [Jesus] has authority on earth to forgive sins.' So he said to the paralysed man, 'I tell you, get up, pick up your mat, and go home!' While they all watched, the man got up, picked up his mat, and hurried away (vv. 10–12).

It's our sins that wreck our relationship with God, and if Jesus can forgive them, as he clearly claimed, then the way is open for us to make a new start with God. St Paul put it this way: 'We were God's enemies, but he made us his friends through the death of his Son' (Romans 5:10).

Jesus offers us the peace of God

There are anxieties and problems in life which are common to us all. Jesus doesn't offer to take them all away. In some ways, following him brings an increase in our struggle, because on top of all the normal things we have to face the pressure of a hostile world and a devious enemy in Satan. What Jesus does promise is that God's peace will come into all these anxieties and pressures, if we trust him. He says:

> So do not start worrying: 'Where will my food come from? or my drink? or my clothes?'... Your Father in heaven knows that you need all these things. Instead, be concerned above everything else with the Kingdom of God and with what he requires of you, and he will provide you with all these other things (Matthew 6:31–33).

The power of God

Change and deliverance from the spirit of powerlessness requires greater power. Jesus demonstrates through his life that he has this greater power. He could heal every kind of sickness (Mark 1:40–44), control natural forces (Mark 4:35–41), order evil powers to obey him (Mark 1:23–27), meet physical needs (Mark 6:30–42) and even bring people back from the dead (Mark 5:21–42).

He brings this same power to work in the lives of those who put their trust in him, changing them and breaking the spirit of powerlessness. He said:

> I am telling you the truth: whoever believes in me will do what I do—yes, he will do even greater things, because I am going to the Father (John 14:12).

Peace with God, the peace of God and the power of God—this is the basis of the new deal which Jesus offers to you. Instead of powerlessness, Jesus is offering you the chance to become a brand new person inside, with a purpose and a plan in this life and eternity guaranteed in the next life. Are you prepared to give this offer some serious thought?

How can Jesus guarantee such things? Before I

answer this question, there is another that men often ask.

Question 3: Does God want men?

This isn't a question central to the Christian faith, but it's a big question for men. We've been brought up with the idea that faith in Christ is for women, or that being a Christian is in some way a soft option. So when we start to think about accepting Jesus Christ for ourselves, we're not just up against a spiritual problem, but a social one as well. I've dealt with this question at length in my book *Manhunt*, so I only want to look briefly at the issue here, but this isn't meant to decrease its importance in any way.

As we read stories in the Bible, it's obvious that men were profoundly impressed with Jesus, and his presence and actions led to remarkable changes in their lives. Jairus (Mark 5:21–43) was a good-living, religious man, faced with a terrible family crisis. His only daughter was at the point of death. In desperation, he came to ask Jesus for help. When he arrived:

> He threw himself down at his feet and begged him earnestly, 'My little daughter is very ill. Please come and place your hands on her, so that she will get well and live!' (vv. 22–23).

Have you, as a man, ever begged anyone for anything? It's unlikely, isn't it, because it's not in our nature. So perhaps you can get an idea of how deeply impressed Jairus was with Jesus, and how he felt quite certain that Jesus could help him.

Peter was a tough fisherman. Impetuous, strong

and quick to speak, he was a real man's man, and he certainly wasn't the sort to surrender his masculinity to anyone. Yet after listening to Jesus and witnessing one of his miracles:

> When Simon Peter saw what had happened, he fell on his knees before Jesus, and said, 'Go away from me Lord, I am a sinful man' (Luke 5:8).

Those are just two of the many men who were changed by the power and personality of Jesus. There are many others—murderers, cheats, the wise, the clever, the able—each one attracted to Jesus like moths to the light, and each one treated as unique and special by Christ. There can be no doubt about it—men were attracted to Jesus and he wanted them to come to him.

He still wants men, and they still respond to his power and love. At an evangelistic meeting recently, a number of women got up in response to the evangelist's appeal, but no men. Then, at the very last moment, a man got up from the middle of the church—a big man, a man's man—and came forward to give control of his life to Christ. When he got to where the evangelist was standing he said: 'I thought I had left it too late and had missed my chance, but I found the courage to come just in time.'

Simon led a very full life, and didn't have much time for religion. He had a nice home and family, a well-paid job with good prospects, and a good social life—he was good at sport. One night his wife gave her life to Christ at a meeting and he immediately noticed the difference in her. For a week he struggled with himself and then, in the middle of the night, rang up the minister of the church to talk it over. The next day in the minister's office he gave control of his life to Jesus. He said: 'I thought I had a full life, but I couldn't get over the change in my wife. I wanted what she had for myself, but I was full of doubts and fears and pride. But in the end I couldn't rest until I had sorted things out with God.'

David gave his life to Christ at a very large meeting, but that was only the end of a long road which started years earlier. He went to church occasionally and one night he and his wife attended a small group in someone's home. There was a discussion about the Christian faith, and some of the church shared their beliefs and convictions. David was touched by what he heard. In his own words: 'As I listened to these people talking about their faith, I realized that there was more to it than just going to church occasionally. I said to myself, "David, there's something different here. Are you going to carry on like you are, or are you going to try and find out what it is they've got?" Now I've found it—or rather him!'

God clearly loves men and wants them to follow him. It isn't a soft option, but it is a deeply satisfying one and a great challenge. But how has Jesus made all this possible? What is it that Jesus has done for the men of his day, and ours?

The Bible explains it to us in this way:

> This is what love is: it is not that we have loved God, but that he loved us and sent his Son to be the means by which our sins are forgiven (1 John 4:10).

Jesus came to be 'the means by which our sins are forgiven', and that turned out to be a very costly experience for him. At a place called Calvary, just outside Jerusalem, he was nailed to a wooden cross which was stuck in the ground, and he was left to die. He experienced real pain, and real blood flowed from a real body. He experienced public disgrace and humiliation in the presence of his enemies, while his friends, including his mother, looked on. Worst of all, at the very end he experienced rejection by God his Father, and cried out from the cross: 'My God, my God why did you abandon me?' (Mark 15:34). As Jesus willingly stood in the place of sinners—our place—he experienced to the full God's anger against sin. All this so that you and I might have a chance to live as God intended. It's hard to imagine this experience, isn't it?

A man who gave his life to Jesus said to me: 'I wasn't really interested in what you were saying, Jim, until you began to describe the physical suffering of Jesus. How could anyone go through all that for me?' If it's hard to imagine the physical experience, then it's even harder to imagine the depth of God's love for us, which lies behind the cross. It's a love that wouldn't give us up, even though we deserved it, a love that would allow Jesus his Son to pass through this agony.

Peter, writing later, described the crucifixion experience, and it might be worth spending a little time reflecting on the implications of what he says:

> Christ himself carried our sins in his body to the cross, so that we might die to sin and live for righteousness. It is by his wounds that you have been healed. You were like sheep that had lost their way, but now you have been brought back to follow the Shepherd and Keeper of your souls (1 Peter 2:24–25).

This is how your sin has been dealt with. How do you feel about Jesus' offer of a new start now? Does it look like a soft option when seen against the agony of the cross?

Question 4: What must I do now?

If after having read this, and perhaps talked with others about it, you feel that you want to become a Christian man, then you must surrender to Jesus. When a fort or a castle surrenders, the doors are thrown open. Those on the outside come in and a new regime takes over. This is what has to happen between you and Jesus—you must open the gates of your life, invite him in and let his authority and rule take over. There's no humiliation in surrendering to someone like Jesus. He's all loving and all powerful, and he wants to share the love and power with you.

When we do accept Jesus into our lives, we have to accept him on his terms. These terms are:

a) Saviour. Recently in England, there was a serious terrorist bombing, and many people were trapped under the debris. One man, who was rescued after many hours, said: 'I found that I was conscious but trapped by tons of rubble. There was nothing I could do but wait. I was helpless. I prayed that someone would come and find me.'

This is how we have to regard Jesus—as someone who comes and helps us because of the impossible position we are in. Jesus comes as our help and rescuer and it's very important for men to understand this because we're often so sure that we can do everything for ourselves.

b) Lord. While my dad was teaching me to drive, he

would sit calmly in the passenger seat and I would fight the beast as best I could! I remember the great sense of relief when, after an hour or so, he would take over and I could sit back and relax. I couldn't understand how he could make something which I found so difficult, appear so easy, but I was glad to let him do it.

When we accept Jesus as Lord in our lives, it's like moving into the passenger seat of the car and allowing him to take the wheel. Just as I was relaxed and confident when Dad took over, so we can be relaxed and confident when Jesus takes over. But only one person can drive at a time, and Jesus insists that he takes over completely. Before you complain or worry about this total take-over, just consider how well you've done so far without him!

Even when Jesus is the Lord of our lives, it isn't all straightforward because there may be many things that we don't want to give him control over, and there may be things that he wants of us that we don't particularly want to do. It takes a lifetime to work all this out, but the commitment to his lordship, to his right to have the final say in all things, must be there in our hearts at the very outset.

Question 5: Can I trust him?

Christ certainly expects a lot from his followers, so for us to ask for some sort of guarantee doesn't seem too unrealistic or unfair. It's also got good Old Testament precedent in the story of Gideon's fleece (Judges 6:36–40). Jesus seems to understand our need for a guarantee, and he left us a very positive one. Shortly before his death we read:

> Then Jesus began to teach his disciples: 'The Son of Man [Jesus] must suffer much and be rejected by the elders, the chief priests, and the teachers of the Law. He will be put to death, but three days later he will rise to life' (Mark 8:31).

Jesus knew about his death and subsequent resurrection, and he shared these facts with his close followers before they happened. They didn't understand what he was saying. So that there could be no misunderstanding, he shared the same facts—death and resurrection—on two subsequent occasions. Then he kept his promise. He was arrested, tried and put to death, but three days later he came back to life again.

There has always been controversy around the question of the resurrection, but to the person of an open mind, the evidence is overwhelming:

a) Something changed a group of defeated men into a dynamic force which swept through the world and has gone on sweeping through it, often in the face of bitter opposition.

b) The authorities and opponents of the Christian faith who were around when the resurrection happened had everything to gain from disproving the claim to resurrection. They also had the best chance (being on the spot). They could have tried to prove that Jesus didn't go to the cross, but that someone else went in his place. They could have said that Jesus only fainted on the cross and revived in the cool tomb; they could have said that the disciples stole the body at night, or that the women had gone to the wrong tomb. But despite having all the advantages, they were unable to disprove the fact of the resurrection.

c) Some of the sharpest brains in the world have

spent two thousand years trying to undermine this claim. They too have failed, and some have become Christians in the attempt—like Saul of Tarsus.

d) Millions of people today, separated by distance, culture and language, believe that Jesus rose from the dead.

Why is the resurrection our guarantee? If Jesus kept this promise, then all his promises can be trusted. So when he claims to speak for God, to have died for our sins, and to be able to offer us life now and for ever, we can trust him.

Question 6: What will happen if I let Jesus take control of my life?

When we surrender to Jesus, we're not in for an easy time. We have to learn to put him first in our lives, to learn about prayer, the Bible, and belonging to a Christian church. These three things alone are quite a challenge, and although there will be Christians around to help us, the intention of our hearts has to be one of willingness to learn these things. Friends and family can make things difficult as well—ridiculing us, treating us as simple or naïve, or dropping us altogether. Lastly, there's the daily pressure of living the way Jesus wants, and not the way the world often demands. There are times when his way can seem very hard.

I'm not trying to put you off—although it might seem like it. But you need to know the whole truth! Following Christ is costly, but there are wonderful compensations:

* Jesus comes to us and promises never to let us go.
* He brings the gift of the Holy Spirit, who gives us the power to live the way Jesus wants us to live.
* He changes us—but at a speed we can cope with.
* We have many friends in the Christian family—people that we would never have known under any other circumstances.

It's a bit like marriage. Sixteen years ago I made a life-changing commitment towards a woman who became my wife. I know much more about her now than I did when I made that great commitment, but all those years ago I knew enough to want to be with her for the rest of my life. The years have shown that I made the right decision.

There comes a point in a man's life when he knows enough about Jesus to be able to make up his mind. Have you reached that point now? If you have, then find a Christian friend and talk it over with him, or find a quiet place, and pray a prayer of surrender to Jesus. Here is a prayer which might be right for you to use:

> Lord Jesus,
> I'm sorry for the past.
> I never realized until now just
> what a mess I have got into, and
> how much I have offended you.
> Thank you for dying on the cross
> for me.
> I surrender my life to you now.
> Come and take control.

Lead me in the way that you know
  is best.
Thank you, Lord.

If you do use this prayer, then ask God to lead you to someone who can help you on from here.

A MAN NEEDS TO GROW MORE LIKE JESUS

Our youngest child is fourteen months old now. When he was born he only weighed six pounds, and I could lift him with one hand. Now it's a major effort to get him off the ground with two hands! No one has taught him about growth, but somehow he seems to have caught on.

However, it's very easy for those of us who follow Christ not to catch on about growth—spiritual growth. New believers can make the mistake of thinking that once they've surrendered to Christ that's all there is to it. More mature believers can make the mistake of thinking that once they've achieved a certain standard of maturity, they can relax and stay where they are.

The truth is that we've never arrived. The experience of growing more like Jesus is a continuing one. Charles Wesley, in a very famous hymn, put it this way:

Changed from glory into glory
Till in heaven we take our place,
Till we cast our crowns before thee,
Lost in wonder, love and praise.

We are to be changed and to grow into the likeness of Jesus day by day. This isn't an optional extra, but part of our experience of Christ. Growth opens up so much to us in our personal lives.

It's the path to satisfaction and maturity

We've come to Christ because we recognize that without him our lives are incomplete and unsatisfying. We're looking for that satisfaction and challenge which he offers, and which will make us the complete men that we long to be. Growth helps us towards this goal. Have you ever thought about how large a goal we are aiming at? It is described for us in this way:

> And so we shall all come together to that oneness in our faith and in our knowledge of the Son of God; we shall become mature people, reaching to the very height of Christ's full stature (Ephesians 4:13).

Christ longs that you and I should be Christlike men. Isn't this a challenge to stir the heart of any Christian man? Isn't this a challenge worth working at—whatever the cost?

It's a sign to our friends

Zacchaeus was a crooked tax collector who cheated everyone in sight. When he surrendered his life to Jesus, he threw a party and invited all his friends to come and meet Jesus. During the party Zacchaeus made this outrageous speech:

> Listen, sir! I will give half my belongings to the poor, and if I have cheated anyone, I will pay him back four times as much (Luke 19:18).

As he had almost certainly cheated everyone at the party, this speech certainly made quite a stir! Maybe the guests wondered just what had got into Zacchaeus, but they couldn't fail to notice the difference in his life. In a very short time, Jesus had brought changes to Zacchaeus' life, and in the same way he will bring changes, which our friends will notice, to ours. After a while, some of them will want to know what it is that has changed us, and the way is open to begin sharing our experience of Jesus with them.

If we're not prepared to grow and change the whole of our lives, it could have very serious consequences for our friends. If we're the same as them then they won't see Christ in us, and as a consequence they could pay an eternal price for our unwillingness to change. Are you prepared to live with this on your conscience?

It's a sign of our obedience

One of the biggest changes that we have to experience as we grow more like Jesus is a change of heart. Without Christ we're often self-centred, arrogant and assertive. We're usually so sure of ourselves, of our abilities and rights. A man surrendered to Christ must have the heart of a servant and this is difficult for us to accept. Jesus has left us his own example so that we can get the right idea. During the last supper, he took a towel and washed the feet of the disciples saying:

> You call me Teacher and Lord, and it is right that you do so, because that is what I am. I, your Lord and Teacher, have just washed your feet. You, then, should wash one another's feet. I have set an example for you, so that you will do just what I have done for you (John 13:13–15).

If Jesus was prepared to serve his own followers, then we too must have the same heart towards those around us—at work, at home, at school, or at leisure. This is perhaps one of the toughest parts of growing and it's bound to be so, because it is so contrary to the ways of the world. But as many have found before us, it is the path to Christian maturity.

I've just touched on some of the results of growth here, and I'll be expanding on these and others later. It isn't easy, but it's a thrilling challenge for any man to take up. It's a lifetime of growth and change, and through it there emerges a better man. Will you accept the challenge of growth, with all that it involves? It might be helpful to spend a few minutes thinking this over, and promising God that he can do as he wishes with you, to make you more like Jesus.

Growth—a practical experience

Running a marathon requires a lot of training on a day-to-day basis. Marathon runners have to be very practical about their training schedule, because if they're not they can't compete properly on the day of the race. Christian men need to adopt the same down-to-earth approach to their growth. It is a daily experience, as God works with us, preparing us for what is to come.

There are certain things that every Christian will need to include in his schedule, and I've outlined them here. If you've only recently surrendered your life to Christ then you might find it better to pick out one or two items that seem important to you. More mature Christians will find it more helpful to work through each item one at a time.

The Holy Spirit and growth

There are two lessons to learn about growth, and we need to learn them quickly. Firstly, it's slow.

My youngest son, Stephen, is crying again! I know why without going to find out. He's learning to walk and it's proving a slow and painful process. But he's getting better at it each day, and in a few weeks he'll be toddling around like the rest of us. Growing as a Christian is a bit like this—slow and occasionally painful, but we get there in the end. We don't do ourselves any good by expecting too much too soon. God takes us along at his speed and we have to be patient. Have you been expecting too much too soon?

Secondly, it's God's work. There's another thing I've noticed about Stephen—he's growing bigger each day. He doesn't read any books about growth, nor does he go to growth classes, but he's still growing. I suspect that one day he'll be like my eldest son—now bigger than his mum and threatening to be bigger than his dad! Children grow from the inside out; naturally, slowly and to a clear plan, and this same principle applies to growing Christians. We grow from the inside out, and it is the Holy Spirit working in our lives that makes this growth happen.

The Holy Spirit comes into our lives when we surrender to Christ. He is dedicated to giving us the strength and ability to grow and develop. We need to learn to draw on that strength, and to let his power into our lives in a fresh way each day. Then we'll grow from the inside out as God works out his plan for us, rather than trying to work it out by ourselves. I use this simple prayer regularly and you might like to use it as well: 'Holy Spirit, come into my life again today. Fill me with your power, and help me to grow more like Jesus.'

Growth and daily surrender

Growth is a daily experience and so is the process of surrendering complete control of our lives to Jesus. Occasionally there are major capitulations, but mostly it's a daily wearing away of the old ways. It's so easy to hold on to some of these old ways, almost without noticing.

This happened to Peter in the Garden of Gethsemane. Even though he had changed a lot since Jesus had first called him, the old arrogance still hung around in the background, and when Jesus warned him of trouble ahead, Peter said: 'I will never leave you, even though all the rest do' (Mark 14:29). Peter was to pay a terrible price for this arrogance, and just a few hours later he denied his Lord three times. If only he had listened and surrendered this corner of his life to Christ.

Are there parts of your life that you're not surrendering to Christ? Why not surrender them now—they're no good to you and will only lead you into trouble.

Growth and God's word

God often shows us his plans for our growth through our daily reading of the Bible. A member of a group which meets regularly in a home to discuss the Bible told this story: 'I read a passage from Mark's gospel one morning. It said: "Jesus came not to be served, but to serve." I didn't think much about it and went off to work. During the morning my boss put a pile of work on my desk that wasn't really mine at all. I thought that he was being a bit unreasonable, and was about to tell him, when I remembered my reading that morning and did the work without complaining.'

Growing as a Christian through using the Bible means more than just reading it—as this story clearly shows. The Bible is one of God's ways of changing our actions and attitudes. We don't have to read it alone of course, and many of us benefit from being in a small group of Christians where we can learn together. When did the Bible last change your daily life?

Growth through listening

A friend of mine came round recently with a problem that he wanted to share. After we had made coffee and sat down, he started, and didn't stop talking for an hour! Every time I tried to say something, he would rush on and I couldn't get a word in. Finally he came to a halt, and giving me an accusing look said: 'Well, you're not much help, I must say. Haven't you got *any* advice to give?'

I was speechless for a moment and then replied: 'Sure I have, and if you would only stop talking for a few seconds I would share it with you!'

I sometimes treat God like this—bombarding him with thousands of questions, and then getting annoyed because he doesn't answer. Maybe there have been times when he has wanted to say: 'Sure, Jim, I've got an answer to your prayer, and if only you would stop talking for a few seconds I would share it with you.'

God does want to answer our prayers. He might guide us by using a verse of the Bible, or through an inner conviction, or through the advice of friends, or through circumstances. But we'll never hear and grow if we don't listen. Do you spend some time during your day just being quiet before God and allowing him to lead and direct you?

Growth into love

Love is an emotional experience, but it has a practical side as well. Even God's love is like this. He loves us deeply, but he puts that love into action:

> God loved the world so much that he gave his only Son, so that everyone who believes in him may not die but have eternal life (John 3:16).

The Christian man who loves God must put his love into action, and this will bring about changes in his life. For example:

* A willingness to take second place to others.
* A willingness to ask for the forgiveness of others.
* A willingness to put up with pain and hurt for the good of others.
* A willingness to love those who aren't particularly loveable.
* A willingness to let attitudes be changed—the aggressions, the self-assertiveness, pride, vanity.

This practical side of love will be very costly to us, and will expose us to ridicule and insult, just as it did Jesus

Christ. To grow in love for others is a very deep challenge to men. Ask God to give you the courage to love more—at home, at work, at play.

Growth into discernment

It's difficult sometimes for Christian men to know where to draw the line. How far can we go along with the ways of the world before they trip us, or before we are seen to be condoning ungodly practices?

The other night I was watching a television programme concerning a citizen's right to resist crime with the use of violence. In one incident, a man was shown violently beating another, and I was horrified by that. My views changed, however, when the commentator said: 'Here we see a father beating up another man who has just raped his ten-year-old daughter.' Now I found myself wanting the father to beat the attacker harder, and I suspect that most viewers would have felt the same. On reflection I'm sure that my reactions were wrong and out of line with what Christ would have expected, yet they seemed so right, and many in the world would have supported them.

This is just a small example of the many difficult moral and ethical decisions that confront a Christian man today. God does make available to us the gift of discernment, and we should be praying regularly for the insight that this gift gives to us, because we're often going to need it. Even so, it isn't always easy to find our way through. Some issues are very complicated and there are no simple black and white answers—however much we might wish there were. The Bible encourages us to look to God and to believe that ultimately he has the answers: 'If any of you lacks wisdom, he should pray to God, who will give it to him' (James 1:5).

There is much more to growing as a Christian than I can include here. A lifetime's experience cannot be compressed into a few pages. If you want to do a little more thinking about Christian growth, here are some suggestions as to how you could go about it. These could provide useful discussion material for a group of Christians. It's often easier for us to tackle these things together, rather than always on our own.

The three-month test

How have you changed in the following areas of your life during the last three months?

a) Power of the Holy Spirit. Do you feel that you know Jesus better now than three months ago? How? If you can see ways in which you know Jesus better, then you are seeing the power of the Holy Spirit in your life. Keep using the 'filling' prayer.

b) Daily surrender. Can you think of things that you've had to surrender to Jesus? What has been the result? Are there areas that still need to be surrendered? Make a note of them now.

c) God's word. Has the Bible had any effect on your daily life at home, work, leisure?

d) Prayer. Has God answered any of your prayers? Can you think of at least three definite examples? This should encourage you to be even bolder in your praying—does it?

e) Love. Have you become more loving towards people—your wife, children, friends? How are you getting along with those you don't like? Think of one of these people and pray for more love towards them.

f) The world. Where do you find it most difficult to follow Christ? Where do the world's ways and his ways clash in your life? Can you find a friend to pray this over with you?

g) Attitudes. Which attitudes have changed and which haven't? Can you think of one incident where you acted differently because you are a Christian?

The one-month diary

Take the points mentioned above and keep a daily record of each over the next month. At the end of the month look over your notes and see if you can spot areas of strength and weakness. Praise God for the strengths and ask for his help with the weaknesses.

Other resources

There are good materials around that can help us to grow. Your local Christian bookshop can suggest books, videos, courses, magazines and so on. Why not go and see what is available.

People

One of the best ways to help our own growth is to talk to others who are ahead of us in the growth process. If you know of more mature Christians, then pester them! Write or phone and ask if you can have an hour of their time to chat things over. We're all in the growing business together, and you may be able to help them as much as they can help you.

A MAN AND THE TOUGH TIMES

Life has some tough times in store for all of us. These can be of short duration, like a sudden illness or a family crisis, or of long duration, like unemployment or terminal cancer. Short or long, these experiences have the potential to blast us, bend us or break us, and do lasting damage to our inner selves. They always provoke the difficult questions like 'why me?' or 'why has God let this happen to me?' Answers, however, are hard to come by.

Christians and non-Christians alike experience the bad times, but respond very differently to them. The non-Christian man is forced back on to the empty platitudes of the world—'it will turn out all right', 'you'll get over it', 'pull yourself together and start to live again', 'have another drink'. Even the most well meaning people can only offer a shoulder to cry on. They're certainly unable to offer the inner healing which is so desperately needed. The Christian man, on the other hand, has many spiritual resources at his disposal which can bring lasting help and healing. Here's an example of what I mean:

Peter and June hadn't been Christians for very long when their church held a Parish weekend at a small conference centre. They both wanted to go, but money was tight, so they prayed: 'Lord, if you want us to go, then please make it possible.' A few days later the money was provided, and seeing this as the Lord's answer, they decided to go. They had a lovely time and learnt a lot about the Christian faith. But when they got home late on the Sunday night, they found that their home had been broken into, and some of their possessions had been stolen. When they had sorted things out, Peter began to reflect. He told me later: 'When I started to think over what had happened, I began to feel anger rising up inside me. I didn't know what it was, but I knew that if I didn't do something, it would spoil the whole weekend. So I prayed: "Lord, please do something to help me with this anger." Almost straightaway I felt the anger disappear, and I've never given it another thought.

Peter had found a way of dealing with this hard experience. It was a way which not only faced the problem, but healed the memory and the upset. A small example of what God can do to help us with the hard times. The same principle applies to all the hard times—both more trivial and more serious. From the great resources of God, I've selected three that have been of great help to me. Careful thought and discussion will bring many more to light. Hard times can be very hard, but can I encourage you to use these and the many other resources that God has for you to use. Perhaps these three will give you an idea of how we can use what God wants to give.

Resources—the people of God

The Bible is full of stories about people who faced and endured the hard times. Reading them can be of great encouragement to us. I have always been encouraged by the prophet Jeremiah. He had a tough job—to warn the people of Judah of their coming judgement—and they didn't like him for it.

Below is a brief account of what he had to endure. It may help you get your troubles into perspective.

* The men of his own town planned to kill him saying, 'Let's chop down the tree while it is still healthy; let's kill him so that no one will remember him any more' (11:19).

* There was a plot to bring charges against him and so silence his preaching (18:18).

* He was beaten and placed in chains by a priest of the Temple (20:1–2).
* He was brought to trial for speaking God's word, and those behind this act were quite brazen. The priests and the prophets seized him saying, 'You ought to be killed for this' (26:8).
* He was banned from the Temple, and his written message was destroyed (36:23).
* He was thrown into a muddy well and left to die (38:6) but was subsequently rescued.
* Finally, he was forced to go into exile in Egypt (43).

All of these trials came to him because he wanted to live God's way and obey God's voice. Yet despite an intense inner struggle and the pressures from outside, he didn't give up. He discovered for himself what the Lord was later to say to St Paul: 'My grace is all you need, for my power is strongest when you are weak' (2 Corinthians 12:9).

Have things got really tough for you? Do you feel like giving up? Why not read through Jeremiah's experiences again, and those of Christ's early followers in the Acts of the Apostles. Ask God to give you added strength. Claim his strength in your weakness.

Resources—the promises of God

Moses was one of God's great men. He was chosen by God to lead the people of Israel out of Egypt, where they were slaves, and into the land God had promised to give them. There were many problems on the journey, but two enemies caused particular concern—

King Sihon of Ammon and King Og of Bashan. Sihon wouldn't let the people of Israel pass through his land, so God said to Moses: 'Look, I have made King Sihon and his land helpless before you; take his land and occupy it' (Deuteronomy 2:31).

Moses obeyed this command and conquered Sihon and his people, but soon afterwards he was faced with exactly the same problem with Og. As Moses hesitated God said, 'Don't be afraid...do the same to [Og] as you did to Sihon the Amorite king' (Deuteronomy 3:2).

It's almost as if God said to Moses: 'Listen, Moses, I told you that if you attacked Sihon, you would win, didn't I? And you did win, didn't you? Now I'm telling you the same about Og. My promise didn't fail you last time, and it won't fail you now. Trust me—and get on with it!' Moses did trust God's promise, attacked Og and beat him.

Moses found that God's promises could be trusted—and God hasn't changed in the three thousand years that have passed since then. His word can be relied on, and what he asks of us is that we both know his promises and trust them.

Millions of us have followed Moses' example and have found our strength in the promises of God. Here are two that have helped me through the trauma of Philip's death and have become very special:

> We know that in all things God works for good with those who love him, those whom he has called according to his purpose (Romans 8:28).
>
> For God has said, 'I will never leave you; I will never abandon you' (Hebrews 13:5).

Do you lean on his promises as I've had to learn to do?

Think back over the last six months. Has God let you down? Let God's faithfulness to you in the past give you courage and strength for today and tomorrow.

Resources—suffering with God

The resources I've already mentioned are a great help to Christians, but our greatest resource is the way that God deals with the tough times and makes us better people through them. He is able to take away the destructive nature of the tough times and make them creative. When he says that all things work together for good, he really does mean *all* things.

The gateway to experiencing this creative resource of God is, strangely enough, the willingness to suffer yet still go on believing that *all* things can work together for good. Jesus was trying to explain this to us when he said: 'If anyone would come after me, he must deny himself and take up his cross and follow me' (Mark 8:34, NIV).

It's hard to put this into words so perhaps I could share in more detail a personal experience I've already referred to. This book is dedicated to the memory of our fourth child—Philip. He was born three years ago prematurely. After the long and trying birth, I had gone home to wash and change, and the hospital phoned to tell me that he had died. He was only a few hours old. I can remember that phone call as if it only happened moments ago—it's engraved on my memory. Mary and I were devastated.

Each day we felt the emptiness more, and when we saw others with babies born about the same time as Philip, our spirits would just faint inside us. Again and again we asked God: 'Why did you let this happen to us?' But as all this was going on, and as we tried to sort out the wreckage of our lives and of our faith, we were beginning to discover a closeness to God that we had never known before. Somehow we could identify more with him—we understood a little of what it meant for him to give up his only Son for us. We were able to understand others better, especially those going through bad times, and they seemed more willing to listen to us. We had earned the right to talk about suffering and pain because we had been there ourselves.

I'm not saying that it's all plain sailing now. For me it's still a long and difficult path—but we can see how the way of suffering and the ability under God to cling to our faith has made us of more use to him. I'm still not totally clear on how we're of more use, but I can see some of the ways.

* Our suffering broke our independence. Until this happened I had always been fairly sure of myself. Now I'm only sure of God.
* Our suffering has thrown us totally onto God. Only he can make sense of the apparent senselessness of life. I remember while I was out walking one day, that I faced a choice. It wasn't whether I would be hurt—that was already decided. The choice was whether I was going to be hurt with God or without him. I chose to be hurt with him.
* Suffering has made us more open to his leading and guiding. We're no longer able to trust ourselves, and we trust him more.

God can see us through the tough times and they can be the most valuable times of our whole lives. I think I've earned the right to say this to you. Pray for those who are suffering, especially if they're men. We haven't always the courage to share how we're feeling.

If you've been hurt yourself, hold tight to God's promise that all things work together for good and ask for the courage to carry on.

3

A Man and His Family Needs

Earlier this year, I had an assignment that took me away from home for quite a long period. Feeling a bit fed up one night I decided to ring home, and my five-year-old answered the phone. As soon as he knew it was me, he came straight out with this question: 'Dad, can Mum go and buy me some chips?' No messing about with all that adult stuff like: 'How are you?' or: 'How long will you be away?' Five-year-olds get straight to the point and, come to that, so do fourteen-year-olds, because on my return from this same trip, as I stood in the hall surrounded by my bags, my eldest son announced in a loud voice: 'And what's more, I don't intend to sleep beneath a pink quilt!' With this cryptic remark, he rushed up the stairs, went into his room and locked the door!

Being a family man, with all its ups and downs, is a rich personal experience. We all want the best for our marriages and our families, but a Christian man wants more than just 'the best'—he wants God's best for himself, his wife and his children. He wants the family to know the love of God daily, and to be guarded and guided by God's creative and positive guidelines. At the end of the day, Christian husbands and fathers want to be able to side with Joshua, who said: 'As for my family and me, we will serve the Lord' (Joshua 24:15).

This intention, although not always easy to carry through, clearly marks out a Christian man's marriage from that of a non-Christian man. As we examine these differences, and the necessary changes that they involve, you might discover areas of your marriage that need to be changed—as I did in writing this book. Are you willing to let God make the changes?

A MAN AND HIS WIFE

Seventeen years ago, on the 23rd August to be precise, I was sitting in the front pew of an Anglican Parish Church. The organ was playing and the church was full of people all dressed in their very best clothes. I turned around, and there at the door was a very familiar woman, dressed in white and carrying flowers. A few minutes later we stood in front of the minister, made our promises and were pronounced 'man and wife'.

It all went so smoothly, and as I was driven to the reception, I remember thinking: 'I'm a husband now, and this is my wife.' But, as I was soon to discover, it isn't a service that makes a marriage, rather it's many years of effort and experience.

It's taken me a long time to realize what a privilege it is to have a good wife. I suppose at first I was too pre-occupied to notice, but that seems a poor excuse. After all, God had already made his feelings clear when he said: 'Find a wife, and you find a good thing'

(Proverbs 8:22). And, 'A prudent wife is from the Lord' (Proverbs 19:14, NIV).

I hope that you've already made this discovery, but important though it is, it isn't the basis for a Christian marriage relationship. Jesus points us to this basic element when he says:

> But in the beginning, at the time of creation, 'God made them male and female,' as the scripture says. 'And for this reason a man will leave his father and mother and unite with his wife, and the two will become one' (Mark 10:6–8).

Christian marriage rests on the conviction that it has a spiritual and an eternal dimension. God is involved in our marriage with us, helping us to understand and follow his timeless guidelines. For the Christian, marriage isn't a question of having a good wife, or conforming to social expectations, but it is following the pattern that God has for us.

This biblical position is up against many challenges today, and non-Christians might be forgiven for thinking that it is an approach to marriage which is outmoded. We live in an age in which the Bible no longer sets the standards for many people, and in which feminism has lowered the esteem of many men so that they no longer even understand what it means to be the head of a household, let alone occupy that position with love and dignity. Recession and unemployment have affected millions of marriages, decreasing the money supply, and making it necessary for many women to work to support or supplement the family income. Even men with jobs are finding that the demands of work limit the amount of time available for their wives and children, and often the time that does remain is not of the highest quality.

Christian women find that the concept of a submissive wife exercised within a loving partnership is not generally acceptable in an age when freedom and liberation are the themes of the day. The security of marriage has been threatened by divorce laws that seem, on the surface, to encourage break up rather than endurance, and the sexual revolution has made fidelity look immature.

What sort of husbands do Christian men have to be, so that their marriages will please God, stand against the uncertainties of the present, strengthen their wives, and show to non-Christians that the biblical concept of marriage, far from being outmoded, is powerful and relevant to today? We're going to look at this question now, and I've chosen to use the term 'servant husband' throughout. This isn't a book designed to boost men at the expense of women. We have a position to occupy in our marriages and it often finds us setting the standards and giving the lead. But we accept this role as servants of our wives, just as Christ came not to be served, but to serve and to give his life for us.

Pause for a moment to thank God for your wife, for all she has done for you and all she means to you. Ask God to give you a servant heart towards her.

I know that many women will read this book, and if you're a wife, pause for a moment to ask God for insight into how he sees your marriage, and what he expects of you and your attitudes and behaviour towards your husband. Your husband can never be a servant husband if you're not prepared to let him and help him.

A servant husband loves his wife

Husbands, love your wives... (Ephesians 5:25).

This is the obvious place to start, of course, and yet we can so easily overlook the obvious—especially if we've been married for quite a number of years. Our marriage is built on the foundation of love for our wife, therefore she must mean everything to us, and her well-being must be our top priority.

This love gets spoilt so easily. Familiarity, the desire for money or success, the ways of the world, the pressures of the children—all these can spoil our first love. We need to do everything in our power to see that this does not happen. Has it happened to you? Try answering these questions honestly:

* Is your wife your very best friend, closest adviser and colleague?
* Do you still love her as much now as you did when you married her?
* When you're away from her, do you long to be with her again?
* Has familiarity bred contempt, or greater appreciation?
* Do you still tell her that you love her?
* When did you last write her a love letter?
* Do you still surprise her with gifts and treats?
* Do you still hold her hand in public?
* Is her well-being of the utmost importance to you?

If you don't truly love her, and you're not totally

committed to her, then you'll never be a servant husband.

The servant husband—as head of his household

> For the husband is the head of the wife as Christ is the head of the church, his body, of which he is the Saviour (Ephesians 5:23, NIV).

Whenever I'm talking about men and marriages, the headship issue is usually the one which causes the most heated discussion. I think this is because people see headship in terms of domination rather than service. The Bible tells us that God has chosen the husband to be the head of the family. This is the divine order of things—however much some might wish that it were different. Our headship, however, is not to be seen in worldly terms but through the eyes of Christ, who although head of the church 'gave himself up for her'. If we want to occupy our headship roles, then we must be prepared to give ourselves up for our wives—to wash their feet, to endure all things for them, to suffer for them, to serve them, to go on loving beyond the bounds of commonsense or infatuation because they mean everything to us. There is to be no limit to what we will do for them.

Denying ourselves for our wives is a tremendous and daunting privilege leaving no room for aggression, dominance or laziness. This is God's way to headship for servant husbands. Have you the courage to walk this way, or to go on walking this way? Perhaps you could talk this over with your wife.

As I was writing these words, Mary was preparing a meal in the kitchen. We had invited some people round for supper with the intention of sharing our faith with them. As I worked, I became aware that Stephen was crying, Paul wanted me to play with him and the older boys were being their usual noisy selves. But surely writing this was more important? A few years ago I would have said so, but times have changed in our marriage. So I switched the computer off, and went and peeled vegetables for the meal. I'm a servant husband now.

The servant husband is considerate

> Husbands...be considerate as you live with your wives, and treat them with respect (1 Peter 3:7, NIV).

When two people live close together day by day, they naturally become very familiar with each other. But there's always the risk that familiarity will breed contempt. Servant husbands must guard against this, and we can do it by respecting our wives. For example:

a) Respect her personality. Our wife is made in the image of God, and we have the privilege of seeing that her personality is developed, not dominated or crushed. Christ trusts us with this responsibility. How are you using this trust? How would you describe the facets of your wife's personality? What are you doing to see that these are developed?

b) Respect her privacy. A wife needs time to herself and the right to keep her thoughts to herself until she is ready to share them. Perhaps occasionally she likes to bath on her own, without her husband coming in to be with her, and she has as much right to good manners and courtesy as any other person. Do you ensure that your wife can have time on her own?

c) Respect her responsibilities. A wife has her unique contribution to make to the marriage and family life.

It's not considerate for a husband to insist on his way in these matters, as this only damages confidence and leads to tension and uncertainty. Do you value your wife's contribution? Do you understand her responsibilities?

d) Recognize her pressures and need for comfort. Being a housewife and mother is a demanding job, and there are tensions and pressures special to this role. If you've ever had to run the house while your wife is away, you'll know just what I mean. Our responsibility is to understand these pressures and to comfort and help her through the very busy moments. We may be tired when we get in from work, and in need of comfort and help ourselves, but if we're going to be servant husbands, then the needs of our wives must come first.

e) Recognize her personal needs. The servant husband has the responsibility to see that his wife has all that is necessary for her personal health and lifestyle. Often she will go without for the sake of the family, and so we have to be even more sure that her needs are met. We might not be able to offer her a Rolls Royce for collecting the kids from school, but has she got enough pairs of tights, make-up, etc? This is not a patronizing position, but just another side of respect and consideration. Working this out is tough, but very rewarding.

The servant husband protects his wife

> Husbands...be considerate as you live with your wives, and treat them with respect as the weaker partner (1 Peter 3:7, NIV).

Women are not spiritually or intellectually weaker than men, but they are certainly vulnerable to abuse from men. This abuse can be physical, emotional or spiritual, and as well as being very damaging to women, it is a very sad comment on the nature of men. In this respect they are 'weaker', and the Bible calls on the servant husband to recognize this fact and to provide protection. He is to provide the creative shield behind which his wife can build the home and become the person that God intended her to be. The servant husband doesn't only hold his wife in his arms in bed, but surrounds her all day as well, in all places and in all circumstances.

The servant husband shares with his wife

> Husbands... be considerate as you live with your wives, and treat them with respect as the weaker partner and as heirs with you of the gracious gift of life (1 Peter 3:7, NIV).

The servant husband is the head of his wife, but this doesn't give him the right to make arbitrary decisions without reference to her. It is part of the subtlety of Christian marriage that the decision-making can be shared, both for the individuals involved and for their corporate life, while at the same time retaining the elements of headship and loving submission.

The servant husband wants the best for his wife

> Charm is deceptive, and beauty is fleeting; but a woman who fears the Lord is to be praised. Give her the reward she has earned, and let her works bring her praise at the city gate (Proverbs 31:30–31, NIV).

The whole of the servant husband concept is undergirded by the husband's desire for the very best—God's best—for his wife. Headship and consideration, respect and protection are all bound up with this concept. What is it that the husband wants for his wife?

a) To be the good wife that God describes in Proverbs 31. Every husband should be familiar with this chapter.

b) To grow into full Christian maturity. The husband wants his wife to 'grow up in every way to Christ, who is the head' (Ephesians 4:15).

If she is going to achieve God's best, then she is going to need encouragement, time and practical help. Then husband and wife can grow together—to mature man and woman, and to mature husband and wife. I must confess that I've only recently begun to appreciate my responsibilities towards my wife in these matters. I regret my failure and I'm slowly learning what I need to do so that she can become the woman God intended her to be. The servant husband I've been describing has not made me feel guilty about my failures, but has helped me to see the direction in which I need to be moving.

We are going to look at some of the practical implications of the servant husband now, but before we do, has the servant husband challenged you in any way? Do you need to go and make a start on some part of your marriage? Or, like me, have you got to go back to the beginning and start again? Promise God that you will do this and ask for his help now.

Christian marriage—making the changes

Changes take time

If like me you've got a lot to undo and rebuild to become the servant husband, then give yourself and your wife time to adjust to the changes. This was a lesson that Mary and I learned through the great custard experience.

We had gone out to lunch with some friends, and Mary had taken an apple pie for sweet. When we got there, she put the pie on the table, along with milk and custard powder, and said: 'I just can't make custard—it always comes out wrong.' In the past, I had a standard remark about Mary's custard, and it wasn't very complimentary. I was on the point of giving it, when I bit my tongue, and said: 'That's not true, darling. Your custard is getting really good now.'

A few days later, we were arguing about something and she said: 'It's all very well you talking about change, but I haven't noticed much change in you.' Then I reminded her about the custard comment, and how I hadn't run her down in front of our friends, because I was trying to stop doing that kind of thing. She had to admit that I was right, and added: 'I suppose I've got so used to you criticizing me, that I find it hard to believe that you really are changing. It takes some getting used to.'

The great custard episode taught us both that changes in marriage take time and need to be handled slowly, with much love and understanding on both sides. Changes also need to be talked through, as they happen, so that both can understand what is happening, and why. Mary and I have spent many hours talking about what is happening to us, and I mean talking—not shouting at each other! Sometimes the hoped for changes don't happen, or don't seem to work out as planned. Then we just get back to talking, and try to make greater allowances for each other. When the custard experiences happen, we can see real change and we're encouraged to keep going.

Many changes have been costly and painful, and occasionally the price has seemed almost too high and we have flared up in frustration or desperation. Sometimes the old ways would look more attractive, and the new ways very difficult to understand. In these times I turned often to Psalm 23, where the Lord reminds us that he is with us in all of life's experiences. In the end, we have had to take our marriage back to God again and again, asking for his understanding and guidance. He has worked changes from the inside and not imposed them from the outside. This has made the changes ultimately joyful, satisfying and rewarding. The last two years of our marriage have been the very best of our lives. Apologies, new attitudes and new insights have led to greater intimacy, greater understanding and greater mutual support.

Many of you reading this may be far ahead of us in this experience. We're only sorry that it took us so long for me to become the servant husband, allowing Mary to be the good wife and mother that God intended from day one of our marriage.

What changes are you longing to see in your marriage? What do you think God has got to change in you so that these changes can begin to happen? Do you expect too much too soon? Do you have time set aside each week, where you and your wife can be alone together, to talk and build the marriage?

Servant head—a way of life

I thought that I was being head of my household, until the cold light of reality dawned on me one morning. A quarrel broke out between the two eldest boys over breakfast, and after a while I stepped in to sort things out. Afterwards, when the boys had left for school, Mary said to me, 'That's what often happens when you're away, and I just don't know how to deal with it.' We spent a long time discussing what she could and should do, and then she said, 'I've never felt before that you were concerned about this sort of problem. You didn't seem to care much, and you didn't correct the children. I felt that I had to do it, and I didn't even have your support.'

This incident made me aware of my shortcomings and forced me into thinking seriously about how I should be leading the family. In the end I realized that headship isn't so much a set of rules and regulations, but much more a way of life. What I do and the way I behave, the way I treat Mary and the others, the way I make decisions and handle discipline—this is my headship. This sets the model for my wife and children, and the patterns of future family behaviour. Once I realized this, I had to make changes in my personal lifestyle so as to set the right example. Do you live a life which sets the right example? Have you earned the right to be the servant head of your wife? Does your wife have any grounds for feeling unsupported, or that someone or something else is more important than her?

At the same time as I was reassessing my role, I had to help Mary understand that I was wanting to take servant headship seriously. We had to talk at great length, until the concept was clear to us, and we're still working through the implications. Does your wife understand how you feel about your headship? Do you understand how she feels about it?

As you have probably guessed, Mary was as much involved in working out the concept of the servant husband as I was—and it will always be this way. A man can't be a servant husband without the co-operation and understanding of his wife. Just as the custard experience helped Mary understand that I was changing, so the earring experience helped me see that she too was willing to make the necessary changes.

While I was away one day Mary had her ears pierced. She did this because she thought I would like it, but I wasn't sure that I did. I didn't say much, which I suppose is saying a lot, but in my prayers that night I said, 'Lord, Mary did this for me. I'm not sure about it. Please don't let me lose my temper like I used to. Please sort this out.'

When we got into bed Mary said, 'I've been thinking things over and I'm sorry about the ears. I realize this is something I should have asked you about first because it affects you as well as me. But I'm having to learn what it means to be a submissive wife, just as you're having to learn what it means to be head of the home.'

This may look like a trivial issue, and in one sense it is, but so much of a deep relationship is built around issues that look trivial on the surface. It was a sign of change for us in our marriage and we thank God for it. Incidentally, I now adore the earrings!

Consideration—our attitude

The other Sunday night, I was getting ready to go to church, as I do most Sunday nights. But as I put on my coat, I noticed that the house needed tidying, the two younger children wanted baths and Mary was looking very tired. In the past, I would have gone off to church and expected supper to be ready when I got in, but on this occasion, I abandoned church in favour of baths!

As the children threw their ducks around and drenched me in water, I realized just how hard it would have been for Mary to do this as well as tidy up and cook supper. For perhaps the first time, I saw things from her point of view, as well as my own, and I think this is the secret of being a considerate husband. Of course it isn't always easy to see things from the feminine point of view, and we need the help of our wives to do it.

Do you ask your wife to explain things from her viewpoint? How does she see you, sex, the family, the home, clothes, God, herself? This can be a very revealing experience and will strengthen your marriage, as well as challenge your view of things, especially if like me you believe that you are always right!

As I've tried this exercise, and tried to be more understanding and considerate, I've come to realize how much tenderness and love need to be part of our relationship. So much of this world is hastle, hustle and hardness. Our wives need demonstrations of tenderness to bring out their nature and confidence. Are you tender towards your wife? Do you show her tender signs of your love and support, for example, with a kiss or caress?

Protection—part of our responsibility

Protecting our wives from physical and mental abuse is really an extension of being considerate, and of seeing things from their point of view. The other day, Mary came home from a visit to the doctors and she was upset. She had managed to lose a lot of weight after Stephen was born, and now she discovered that the lure of cakes had put it all back on again! Instead of coming out with all my standard comments like 'it doesn't matter', or 'pull yourself together', I put my arms around her, and said, 'Look, we can face this together. Get the diet sheet out again, and let's get back to lettuce and apples!'

This is a small example of protection, and I'm finding more and more that I can protect Mary without patronizing her in any way, or treating her as a child. Do you see yourself as a protecting husband? Do you let your wife go out alone after dark? Do you let her housework get on top of her without intervening? Do you let your children abuse her without giving some protection and instruction? It's a privilege to protect—are you accepting it?

Sharing together

I'm an outgoing person, but I keep my inner feelings very much to myself. This makes it hard for people to get to know the real me, and has made it difficult for Mary in the past. But if our marriage is going to be as God wants it, then there has got to be a real sharing of the real us. We've started to do this, but it hasn't been easy. As I've shared myself with Mary, she has discovered what a weak and insecure person I am, and I'm not sure that she's always liked this side of me. I remember one day we were discussing our inner feelings together, and she said: 'Well, I don't like you the way you are!' I replied, 'What do you expect me to do about it? This is what I'm really like. You said you wanted to know me, and now that you do, you don't like it!'

We've found however that the truth makes the best basis for a marriage, and leads to real growth and change.

Have you been sharing the real you with your wife, and has she been sharing the real her with you? There are short-term problems, but great long-term benefits. Have you the courage to start, or to go further if you've already started?

Sharing demands courage and time—top quality time. It's no good thinking we can build real sharing relationships in an odd five minutes here and there. But so often that is all we have left at the end of a long day, before we fall exhausted into bed. Finding good quality time can be difficult, especially if there are children in the house. But despite all the problems, time can be found if we really consider it to be important. A baby-sitter might cost a few pounds, but it gives you a few hours together. Perhaps the children could go out to tea, or watch TV in one room for half an hour while you sit down to coffee and chat in the kitchen. It depends how important finding the time is to you. Is it important?

Wanting the best

I'm just about to take sole charge of the family for a full six hours! Mary is going to a women's day of prayer and discussion, and I'm in charge. That doesn't sound too spectacular, but what is unusual about it is that I've suggested that she go. In the past she would make the suggestion and all the arrangements, and I would go my own sweet way. But now I want the best for her, and I'm on the look-out for events and opportunities that will benefit her, and if I have to work harder for that day or evening, then I'll do so willingly.

It isn't always spiritual events I encourage her to attend. She had a day out recently with some friends, and again I looked after the family. She really enjoyed herself, and so did I. We had a real man's day—seaside, fun park and chips! If you want the best for your wife, then start looking around for opportunities which will help and encourage her, and develop her potential under God. This can be a very satisfying experience—are you enjoying it?

Servant husbands need understanding wives

A servant husband needs the support and encouragement of his wife as he takes on the privileges and responsibilities of his position. How can a wife help her husband?

Pray for him

I hope this book has given wives a better understanding of their husbands. This understanding needs to be turned into prayer. Try to determine your husband's particular needs, and pray regularly for him. If you share regularly together, this is obviously easier, but even if you don't, you should be able to spot the areas of need yourself.

Understand what the Bible says about husbands

Wives will be better placed to help if they have a clear understanding of what God is expecting of their husbands. So spend time trying to understand God's rule for husbands. Read through what has already been said, and look up the references. How do you think your marriage is shaping up in the light of them? God also expects you to be a good and submissive wife. Are you? Your husband can never be the husband God intended if you are not willing to match him as the servant wife. Does your husband have any reason to be ashamed of you? Are you in any way undermining him? Are you willing to accept his advice, guidance, consideration and protection? Do you share yourself with him?

Be patient

Many wives come to speak to me after I have spoken at meetings about and for men. Most of them feel that their husbands are not servant husbands, and want to know what they can do about it. Perhaps the hardest lesson that these women have to learn is that they must be patient. Often wives pester their husbands, but this only has the reverse effect—they just become more obstinate.

It takes time for men to change, so give your husband time, room to think and experiment, and the privilege of making mistakes as he tries to change.

Christian wives—non-Christian husbands

This is one of the most pressing problems in the area of men's work. Again and again, women ask me: 'My husband doesn't know the Lord—what can I do?'

There's no easy answer of course, but often I feel that these women have been abandoned by the Christian men of their fellowships. Often they are left to struggle on alone, trying to win their husbands for Christ, when it's really the job of the Christian men of the church or fellowship to do this. For the Christian women who are in this position, and are reading this book hoping to get some idea of what to do, here are a few practical suggestions to help you along the path of making your husband a Christian man.

He is still your husband

It's so easy for a woman in this position to look with envy at other wives with their Christian husbands, and to think: 'If only I had married Tom,' or, 'If only we could be like Mary and Jim.' But the Bible is quite clear—the man you married is your husband, and:

> In the same way you wives must submit to your husbands, so that if any of them do not believe God's word, your conduct will win them over to believe (1 Peter 3:1).

Your husband is your husband, whether he believes or not, and God expects you to fulfil the role of the submissive servant wife, despite his unbelief. This is an extremely difficult position in some circumstances, but if you want him to believe, it's an essential ingredient. Are you a submissive servant wife to him?

Do not give up on him

Your love and obedience to your husband, and to Christ, have an eternal significance for him. There are many women in this land, and beyond, who know that God has answered their prayers for their husbands, even though they have had to pray for many many years. You may have to pray and wait for thirty or forty years, but nothing is impossible with God. Are you prepared for this kind of prayer and patient commitment?

Don't isolate him

One of the biggest dangers facing you is that your husband should have reason to believe that he's in competition with the church for your time and love.

To prevent this happening, you may have to miss church or church events from time to time, to be with him. A works dinner, a trip to the seaside with the kids, a leisurely Sunday breakfast together—all help him to see that he's not in competition for your love. Has he ever had grounds for feeling this?

At the same time, be careful not to isolate him from church things. Make sure that you include him in as many events as possible. Choose events that he might like—picnics, work days, concerts, videos, etc.

Don't go it alone

In my experience, bringing a man to Christ is a long job. So you are going to be faced with a long period of prayer and patience. God never intended that we should have to handle these experiences alone. Look for a Christian friend who will join you in prayer for your husband. If you can find a woman who is in the same position as you—or has been—then she will pray with understanding. Why do it alone? God never intended it that way. Or are you too proud to ask for help and support? If you're tempted to give up, and you will be, remember that unknown to him, your husband is depending on you.

A MAN AND HIS CHILDREN

By now you will probably have gathered that I'm a family man. Mary and I had only been married about a year, when she began to have this strange morning sickness. In those days we didn't know what it was, or what it meant. Four children later, we're familiar with the symptoms and the cause! Our children are all boys and we love them dearly. We've come to recognize the joy and privilege of having a large family.

Over the last few years, as Mary and I have been reshaping our marriage, I've had to relearn what it means to be a Christian father. It has not been easy—especially for the children who have had to experience a change of attitude and expectation. However, it has been worth it and some of the changes have begun to filter through our daily lives. Mary said recently, 'Even our children have started saying "thank you" for their meals now.'

The changes I have made are based on God's plan for fathers, and I've chosen the title 'loving father', as this seems to capture for me the very heart of God's intention for fathers and their children.

The loving father loves his children

> Dear friends, let us love one another, because love comes from God (1 John 4:7).

Adult Christians are constantly being encouraged to love one another, and rightly so. God's expectation is that we offer this same quality of love to our children. This is love of the highest quality. It refuses to give up, whatever the cost. It's the same quality of love which led Christ to his crucifixion. It is love which is willing to go on being hurt again and again, but at the same time goes on forgiving for ever.

It's so easy to stop loving with this quality of love when faced with an arrogant teenager, or an erring and unrepentant adult son or daughter. It's so much easier to wash the feet of the world rather than the feet of our children. Yet if we cannot do this for them, how can we ever hope to do it for the world?

When we are feeling frustrated, exasperated or bewildered by the children—and this happens to all parents—we would do well to remember that they didn't ask to come and be members of our family. They are our choice, and since we chose them we should be prepared to love them always.

The loving father loves his wife

> Husbands, love your wives just as Christ loved the church and gave his life for it (Ephesians 5:25).

One of the greatest gifts a father can give to his children is a secure marriage, where genuine love is shown between him and his wife. As the husband and wife work the loving relationship out, as servant husband and wife, so the children will see something of God's love for them mirrored in the parents' relationship. As parents, we have the chance to help our children gain an idea of what real love is—as a counter to the distorted love that the world shows them daily.

A loving father gives his children time

> Call to me, and I will answer you; I will tell you wonderful and marvellous things that you know nothing about (Jeremiah 33:3).

God is ready to make time for us whenever we are ready to make time for him. His promise is, 'Call, and I will answer.' He doesn't say: 'Call, and I might answer,' or, 'Call, and I will answer when I can spare you five minutes.' The God of the universe, the Lord of lords and King of kings, is ready to make time for us anywhere and anytime.

God expects us to treat our children in the same

way. They can have time from us anywhere and anytime. A few spare minutes out of our lives just isn't enough. They need top quality time and they've a right to expect it. This may be costly to us, but it does have enormous advantages. Time spent in this way builds trusting relationships and opens the way for genuine guidance and sharing. It will also help us to avoid the mistake of expecting too much from our children, or expecting them to fulfil our ambitions. Time allows sharing of hopes and fears, and allows parent and child to be themselves within a trusting relationship. This is all going to cost you time—but isn't it worth it?

The loving father trains his child

> Teach a child how he should live, and he will remember it all his life (Proverbs 22:6).
>
> Fathers, do not exasperate your children; instead, bring them up in the training and instruction of the Lord (Ephesians 6:4, NIV).

We live in an age of free expression and non-directive counselling. We're encouraged to find things out for ourselves and while this is not a bad thing, God doesn't see parenthood in this way. He clearly expects us to teach and train our children in his ways and the responsibility for giving this direction is laid on the shoulders of the head of the home, even if he shares this privilege with his wife. We are expected to give advice, guidance, instruction and discipline where necessary. But God expects us to do this in the most natural and appropriate way. We're not to irritate, exasperate or demoralize our children, but to give positive and creative guidance with a gentle spirit. To do this we are going to need considerable diplomacy, skill and patience.

The loving father welcomes his children home

> [The son] was still a long way from home when his father saw him; his heart was filled with pity, and he ran, threw his arms round his son, and kissed him (Luke 15:20).

At the end of the day, if we really love our children then the welcome mat will always be out for them, no matter what they've said or done, whatever problem they've come up against, or whatever mistake they have made. Children will stray, but they must always know that they are welcome home. Is this your basic attitude? If it isn't, then you'll never be the loving father of the Bible. If it is, then your children will never go far wrong.

This concept of the biblical loving father is not meant to lower the value of Christian mothers. They have a unique contribution to make to bringing up the family as they work with their husbands. But the real challenge is to the Christian husband—the challenge to take up his headship position and to take the lead in standards, discipline and training.

Mary and I have been trying to put some of these ideas into practice, and as we have done so, we've learnt some practical lessons which might be of use to others.

Loving our children

Our love for our children has to show itself practically and in many different ways. With the young ones it takes the form of lots of personal affection—especially from me. They're used to getting it from Mum, but we want them to grow up knowing that Dad loves them as well. A story at bedtime, the occasional treat and a genuine interest in their world is what is required. The attitude in my heart is quite simple: God loves me so I want to love them in the same way. Is this your attitude?

With the teenagers it's a very different story. Love isn't just the treats and advice, but it also shows itself in a genuine desire to understand their world rather than remain in ignorance. Their world is very different from ours. Have you ever stopped to consider how different? In our world, attitudes are fairly well formed, values fixed and expectations clear. Our world is relatively settled, but theirs is in turmoil with fluid values, strong peer group pressures and conflicting needs to rebel and to conform at the same time. I'm glad I don't have to grow up surrounded by these pressures—I think I would have a lot of trouble. No wonder my teenage children get irritated with me, or angry at my apparent conservatism or reactionary behaviour. I've tried to understand their world, and I would encourage you to do the same, because it really gives value to our love and concern for them. Don't become like parents who say to me, 'You can't teach us much about teenage kids—we've got them ourselves.' Having teenagers yourself is only the beginning of understanding. There are many good books in the library, teenage magazines and TV programmes that can help you. Trained youth workers in the community, various courses and your own teenagers can be a great help, if only you will have the humility to let them. The Bible tells us that love is only happy with the truth. Are you willing to make the effort to find out the truth about being a teenager today?

There's also the other side—of introducing them to our world with all its responsibilities and opportunities. Are you trying to help your teenagers into this adult world? Perhaps you need to start sharing some of your decisions with them—things that you would normally decide for yourself. Perhaps you might even ask: 'What would you do in these circumstances, David?' Who knows, they might even come up with an answer that you had not thought of, and it may be of great help to you. Real love is a two-way process after all.

Real love for our children means we'll want to transform them over a period of years from dependants to friends. Are you beginning to regard your older children as your friends—people you like to be with and share with? More importantly, do they regard you as a friend, someone they are proud to know and enjoy being with? This unique friendship comes when two people with contrasting lifestyles and outlooks are willing to share their lives together. This can only happen within the context of love and we, as fathers, are expected to make the running. How are you getting on? How do your children think you are getting on? Have you asked them lately?

Giving them time

The other night I came in at about 6.00 p.m.—really tired after a hard week—and the armchair looked very inviting. I was just about to sink down into it with a cup of coffee when Paul said, 'Want to come and play cricket, Dad?' I groaned inwardly, but I agreed to go. Mary said to me, 'Why are you going? You could do with a rest.' But I replied, 'I'm going because my children are entitled to some of my time. I'm giving them time that I would rather have for myself.'

Are you giving quality time to your children—time that you would like for something else—rather than trash time? When did you last give them a whole hour of your undivided attention?

Of course you don't have to sit down and say, 'OK, boys, let's have some quality time together.' Be imaginative—games, walks, places to go to all make good use of time together. Our is a very male-orientated house, so for us it's motorbikes, the hamburger house, the chip shop and football. It doesn't matter what it is, as long as it's for them.

As well as our time, children need time to themselves and time with their friends. Sometimes it's inconvenient to take them to a friend's house or pick them up from a club or sport, but out of love for them and respect for their time, shouldn't we do it? They need time alone as well, to rest and think. When your children sit down with that vacant look on their faces, do you always say, 'Why are you sitting there doing nothing? Find something to do!' This seems a bit tough on them when they see us adults doing that very same thing. If we need rest time, so do they, don't they?

Giving training to our children

When Mary went for her first ante-natal check at the hospital when we were expecting Stephen, I was a bit worried. My mind kept going back to Philip—we had been through all this then, but he had died. David came with us to the hospital, and while he and I were waiting, I shared with him the things that were worrying me. I don't know why, but it just seemed right. He was my eldest boy, and I felt that he was enough of a friend to listen. He was very understanding, and I hope that what he heard will be useful to him if and when he has to sit alone in an ante-natal clinic waiting for his wife.

This little incident captures for me the real meaning of the biblical instruction to train a child in the way he should go. Like headship, training is not a series of lectures on what is right or wrong. It's rather a sharing of my life with my children, so that they have a model on which to build their own lives. Do you let your children into your life and allow them to see your struggles? Or do they think that you've got it all right, and that they are the only ones with problems? Is this good training for their future lives? We've taken to sharing more and more of ourselves with our older children for this very reason. Have you?

Part of the training process is the willingness to admit mistakes and say sorry—and this is a two-way process. Yesterday, I blew up at John for some trivial reason, and although I felt I was right I went and apologized to him. I expect him to do this to me, and the best way of helping him understand this is for me to do it to him. We have become a 'sorry' house, and we believe that this helps equip the children to face the inevitable failures and mistakes they will make in later life. Failures and mistakes are allowed in our house, and we have a mechanism for dealing with them—how about you?

Another important area is 'thank you', and we're becoming a 'thank you' house too. This builds self-esteem and confidence. The other morning, there was a loud crash outside our bedroom door, and we rushed out to find breakfast cereal, toast, tea and china everywhere. In the middle of the wreckage was John, who had tripped on the stairs while bringing up our breakfast. Immediately we both thanked him for his generous idea, and set about picking up the bits. As soon as we had thanked him, his face lit up, his confidence was restored, his gift was noticed and appreciated, and to our amazement even his elder brother helped clear up the mess—wonders will never cease! We could have complained about the mess—but why?

Are you a 'thank you' house? Do you appreciate what your children do for you, even if the things they do don't always work out quite right?

Being a 'thank you' house doesn't stop me taking a firm line on discipline when necessary. It's important that children should know where the lines are drawn, and which punishments will come as a result of which actions. But discipline needs to be fair, fairly applied and done out of love, not anger or hate.

The other day, David came out with a mouthful of bad language, and I sent him to his room for the evening. It was hard for me not to change my mind and let him off, but I stuck it out. Next morning, I took him a cup of tea and gave him a cheery 'good morning'. Once the point has been made, that's it as far as I'm concerned. On this occasion that was also it as far as David was concerned. There's to be no grudge or lingering resentment on either side.

Is your discipline fair? Are you too lenient or too harsh? How do your children feel about it? Do you see it through out of love?

Our expectations

What do we expect from our children as they grow older? It's so easy to use them to overcome our past failures or missed opportunities.

Many parents seem determined to make their children learn to play the piano, and the kids practise for hours at something they might not particularly enjoy because their parents feel it's good for their development. Is this the truth? Or is it that they want them to learn the piano because they failed to learn it?

The same question has to be asked about school work. Children need to be encouraged to do their work of course, but are we pushing them for their own good, or are we pushing them because we want them to achieve what we failed to achieve? Each of us is made unique by God, and our job as parents is to encourage our children to find in themselves what God has put there, not to impose on them what we want to see. It's a delicate balance. What are your expectations for your children? Are they fair?

A MAN AND HIS PARENTS

I've been very fortunate in having wonderful parents, but this is not true for everyone. However, whether the relationship is a good one, or not so good, the Christian man has responsibilities towards his parents and in-laws. The Bible gives us some guidelines.

The caring son makes a clean break

> For this reason a man will leave his father and mother and be united to his wife, and they will become one flesh (Genesis 2:24, NIV).

The Christian man has the responsibility to see that a clean break is made with his parents, and those of his wife, when a marriage is formed. This is not to be done in arrogance or pride, but is the clear biblical injunction and leaves the way open for a brand new relationship between parents and married children. The break is made in order to let something better and more lasting emerge, not in order to escape. The period of engagement gives all concerned the chance to prepare for the coming changes. If we don't make the break, we're out of line with God, and in for troubled relationships. Have you made the break?

The caring son continues to care

> Honour your father and your mother, so that you may live long in the land the Lord your God is giving you (Exodus 20:12, NIV).

God obviously takes parenthood as seriously as he takes marriage. He expects us to go on honouring our parents for as long as necessary—he sets no time limit. 'Honour' has the connotation of respect and dignity, of trust and value. How can we carry out this responsibility towards our parents and in-laws in a caring way?

a) We must be prepared to spend time with our parents, just as we spend time with our wife and children. Time builds trust. When did you last give quality time to your parents?

b) We must accept that within our marriage relationship God expects us to build, or try to build, a deep relationship with our parents—not a casual or uncommitted one. How would you describe your relationship with your parents?

c) We are not entitled to abandon our parents, however much they may seem to deserve it. This is difficult for many, but at least we can go on writing to them, phoning them and praying for them.

d) We must not dictate to them. When parents get old, it's so easy for us to feel that we have all the answers to their problems because we're younger and fitter than they. But they are people in their own right and if they seem to follow what appears to us to be strange ways, we may wish to discuss it, but in the end they must make the decisions because they have to live with the consequences. The caring son knows when to say no, and when to leave well alone.

How well are you working things out with your parents? Your attitude as the husband and head of the home will set the standard not only for your wife but for your children in later years. This is a serious headship responsibility—are you accepting it?

If things are really fine between you and your parents, and if they have a real place in your marriage, then pause to thank God because you are very fortunate.

4

A Man and His Daily Life

Men are basically private people. We're not given to showing our emotions, or talking about our private feelings unless the circumstances are exactly right. So it is possible for us to accept the lordship of Christ in our personal and spiritual lives without necessarily making this too apparent to others.

It is also possible for us to be private in our marriages and in our family lives. We can easily hide our problems so that others cannot see through our pretences. In my years as a minister, I've never ceased to be amazed and saddened when marriages which I thought were solid and secure come to an end. I'm obviously not very good at seeing through the pretence —or perhaps those involved have been very good actors.

But in our daily lives—at work or at leisure, at church or with friends—there is no chance of us being able to stay private Christians. In our daily lives we are constantly mixing with non-Christians, working close to other philosophies, other ways of doing things, other styles of decision-making, other values and other expectations. Here we cannot hope to stay private

Christians, and why should we want to anyway? This interaction with the world is possibly the most exciting and thrilling part of our lives. It is here that our faith is tried and tested, and where others will see the Christian difference, and hopefully begin to evaluate Christ for themselves. Our daily lives force us out of our buildings and cosy fellowships and give us the chance to stand for Jesus. This was clearly his intention, when he said to his followers: 'Go, then, to all peoples everywhere and make them my disciples (Matthew 28:19).

It's in our daily lives that we live out this command, and although it's often tough for us at work or as unemployed men, this is where our fighting qualities come to the front. Some churches and fellowships obviously haven't grasped this message, and seem to regret our daily involvement with the world. At one church, a man was encouraged not to join his union, even though he felt that as a Christian he should be seen to be involved. The problem was that the union met on a Sunday morning in the local hotel and consequently he would miss attending church once a month.

Sadly, many ministers and full-time workers seem to have little idea of what it means to work in industry, commerce or the caring professions, and do little to familiarize themselves, and this makes it difficult for the majority of men. But the Lord is behind us. He sends us out into the world where our faith will be tested and will grow. Some churches have more vision of course. At one church, a man was positively encouraged to get involved in local hospital radio, even though this would mean his absence from Sunday evening worship.

Have you ever been tempted to see your daily life as

an inevitable but boring experience that has to be got through as quickly as possible? This dishonours God, and is a disaster as far as your non-Christian friends are concerned. Your daily life is your mission field—where God has put you to work for him. Will you ask him to help you see things from this point of view—wherever you find yourself day by day?

As we consider together how we are to live out our daily lives as surrendered men, it's important to remember why it is that we want to do it at all.

We are not doing it for personal glory

Living the Christian life brings great satisfaction to us and hope to others. There's nothing wrong with enjoying the satisfaction, but we must not forget that this is not the purpose of living Christ's way—only the spin off. It's so easy to move from satisfaction to pride. I know because I've done it myself. We would do well to recall the parable of the servant, which finishes with these lines: 'We are ordinary servants; we have only done our duty (Luke 17:10).

We are doing it for his glory

This is the real motive for Christian living. I only continue trying to live out my faith because I know that this is God's plan for my life, and by living to the plan, my humble and inadequate life will bring glory to him. Often I want to give up because those who live by other standards seem to do so much better than me, both morally and financially. Have you ever felt like this? Have you ever felt like giving up? This is why it's so important to remember that we are living for his glory and not our own. No matter how much we stumble around, God will not let his name be dishonoured. As long as we are jealous for that name, and not our own, things will work out right in the end.

Others are depending on us

As Christian men, we lose sight of the effect that our faith has on other people. But I'm convinced that others do evaluate the Christian faith according to the way we behave. Our faithfulness may be the means of bringing some of them to Jesus.

Recently I was leading a discussion on Jesus in a large comprehensive school. I say 'leading' but in fact some of my listeners were getting the better of me, and I must have looked a fool. However, I was conscious of some very quiet, intense faces watching me all the time. I felt like giving up because of the hostility, but those intense faces kept me going. Even if only one of them found Jesus as a result of the battering I was taking, then that made it all worth while.

If there is anyone in your daily life who has got their eye on you, and I'm sure there is, then if you give up who will help them? They are depending on you.

A MAN AND HIS DAILY LIFE-WORK

I want to look first at the Christian man and his paid work, and later I'll look at the life of the Christian man who doesn't have paid work. I live in an area where many men are without paid work, but this doesn't make them useless or unemployable, so I'm not going to use the degrading term 'unemployed'.

Paid work is the place where, for many of us, our faith is tried and tested. There are many issues to face daily:

* Moral issues.
  How do I behave? What do I say and do?
* Ethical issues.
  What is the difference between a gift and a bribe?
* People issues.
  How do I treat others and how do they treat me?
* Commercial issues.
  How does the business keep afloat, and what is permissible to make this happen?
* Satisfaction issues.
  How do I get the best from work?
* Home issues.
  How do work and home fit together for the benefit of both?

Work environments can be very tough for Christian men. I've just finished a series of meetings in large comprehensive schools, and I've great sympathy for Christian teachers. It's hard to keep moving forward for Christ in the face of low morale, limited resources and disinterested kids who face a very insecure future. There are many other comparable situations in our land today, with stress, boredom, insecurity and feelings of injustice making life very difficult.

It can be tough for Christian workers *and* Christian management. A man on the shop floor might find it hard to stand against obscene language, and likewise a man in management might find it hard to face making men redundant, or to handle a deal which is only just legitimate.

There are lonely jobs, dangerous jobs, isolated jobs, dirty jobs and pointless jobs. Being a man at work has always had its challenging side, and many of the problems are not just common to Christian men. It is hard for many non-Christian men facing the issues of work today. I wouldn't want to undermine or undervalue those who, while not believing in the risen Christ, still want to work honestly, to improve the common lot and stand against moral and ethical corruption.

So, if we're in the same struggle, what is the difference between us? The Bible makes it clear that the Christian worker has a different intention: 'We make it our goal to please him' (2 Corinthians 5:9, NIV). Christian men are working for a different employer and have a different set of aims and objectives.

a) We want to capture our workplace for Christ. Despite all the obstacles, any lesser aim will dishonour the Lord. How we go about this task is another matter, but we need this objective written clearly across our hearts. Perhaps part of the church's failure to reach men is that ordinary Christian men haven't been encouraged in this aim. It's time for a change of attitude.

b) We bring our spiritual resources to bear on our place of work—prayer, the Bible, our home fellowship, Christ's inner presence. This gives us some equipment to deal with stress, success, failure, competition, apparent injustice and pressure from home.

c) We are accountable for everything we do or say. We haven't the option of deciding how to behave, because we are always found out by Christ. A non-believer can choose to do right or wrong and hope to get away with the consequences. We never get away with it, so we're delivered from even trying.

There are many different types of work, and if we're in work then we're all at different levels of responsibility and accountability. So let's look at the Bible to see if there's a general picture of the sort of men we're expected to be at work. I've chosen the title 'accountable worker' because we are accountable to Christ for our work.

The accountable worker is a man of integrity

We will never find a better man (Genesis 41:38).

The patron saint of integrity must be Joseph (Genesis 37–46). Hated by his brothers, sold into slavery, insulted by his owner's wife and forgotten by those he had helped, he was finally called into the presence of the King of Egypt to interpret a dream that the king had experienced. Interpreters of dreams sometimes paid for their explanations with their lives, and this dream wasn't a comfortable one predicting as it did famine for the land. But Joseph wouldn't be put off by the risk. First he gave the credit for the interpretation to God. He said he was unable to give an interpretation himself, but that 'God will give a favourable interpretation' (Genesis 41:16).

Then he interpreted the dream without any apology or concession. In Joseph the king saw a man to be trusted, a man who wouldn't pull back from his duty, whatever the cost, and said: 'We will never find a better man than Joseph, a man who has God's spirit in him (Genesis 41:38).

This is exactly what our employers and workmates should say about us, and when they do, we must give the glory to God. We have to be seen to be honest, morally correct, reliable, and unafraid of facing the hard issues with fairness and compassion. This doesn't make us soft people who are an easy touch, but it does make us men of God.

We do need to be clear about what the issues are, and where we stand on them. Here are some areas that need decision and some questions that need facing. Have you faced them?

a) Is there a difference between private use of the company phone, taking a few hours off without permission and taking small amounts of material home on the one hand, and malpractice and bribery on the other? Where do we make our stand, for how long and in what style?

b) How do we live with conflicts of the profit motive, pressure from and on colleagues, conflict with the home *and* at the same time remain human beings with a respect for others with whom we work despite their behaviour?

c) What is the right attitude to an employer—total surrender, total arrogance and resistance, or some middle way?

d) Are there some changes that you need to make? For example:

* Have your attitudes hardened?
* Are there some apologies due?
* In humility, are you a Christlike man?
* Do you pray for change in your colleagues and workmates?

Changes in our work environment don't happen overnight. It takes perseverance, and there are many painful experiences on the way. It's so easy to reach the point of not bothering any more. Have you reached this point? Is it time to change your thinking and your attitude, and to make a new beginning? If it's been a long hard struggle for you, and still is, then read the story of Daniel's struggle, and the results (Daniel 6).

A modern-day Daniel might easily be my friend Joe. For years he had been trying to talk to his shift foreman at work about Christ, but things never worked out. So Joe just got on with his job, trying to live out his faith at his workbench. When the local church had a men's night in the pub, Joe invited his foreman, and to his amazement, he came. When Joe met him the day after the event, the foreman said, 'I must know the name and address of that speaker. What he said about God has given me a lot to think about—in fact I haven't stopped thinking about it the whole weekend.' Joe was delighted. What was it that had brought this foreman to the pub night? The years and years of Joe's honesty and integrity. The same could be happening at your place of work at this very minute.

The accountable worker is a man of prayer

In everything by prayer (Philippians 4:6, NIV).

The Bible is full of stories about praying men and women, and of God's answers to those prayers. We follow in their praying footsteps and if our faith is really central to our everyday life, then the events of our working life should occupy quite a bit of those prayers. If we limit our prayers in any way, then we are the ones who have placed the limit. God has made his position clear: 'Do not be anxious about anything, but in everything, by prayer and petition, with thanksgiving, present your requests to God' (Philippians 4:6, NIV).

His command is that we present our requests to

him—requests from every part of our lives. He's prepared to be concerned with the troubles of the Middle East and the shortage of screws on your production line and the breakdown of relationships in your office. This is the nature of the God we follow, and as we let others see that we pray about our work, so he will begin to become real to them.

Do you pray throughout your working day for the people around you, those you speak to on the phone, the problems and joys of your corner of the paid working world? Do you pray for honest dealings by your employers, for justice in the firm, for willingness to be compassionate and understanding? Do you pray for your products; that they will be of good quality, useful and won't in any way harm the users? Do you pray for those operating heavy machinery, for their safety and health? A man of prayer is one for whom all these things—and many others—are as natural as breathing.

The accountable worker is a man of compassion

> The Lord is merciful and good; our God is compassionate (Psalm 116:5).

There is a lot of competition and hardness at work, and being men we're not given to showing tenderness or understanding. Yet as surrendered Christian men, we should be noted for our compassion. In the parable of the Good Samaritan, the man who receives the commendation of Jesus is: 'The man who was kind' (Luke 10:37).

We are to be this sort of man at work—a man who shows mercy, compassion, understanding and tolerance to his fellow workers. Are you known as this kind of man? There are so many at work who need our understanding.

I was on a course once with twelve other men, and one of those with us was much older and more experienced than the rest of us. Consequently, we took a dislike to him, but to my credit I tried all I could to resist this general dislike, although I found it difficult. One day I arrived early for a session and he was sitting alone. I asked him how he was, and he said, 'Jim, I'm at my wits' end. My wife's mother has been seriously ill for these last weeks, and we just don't know which way to turn.'

I felt awful. There we were making this man's life uncomfortable, when all the time he needed compassion and understanding.

How many similar stories could be true of the people at your place of work?

How do we show Christian concern and compassion? Here are some possible ways:

* By making our own mind up about people and not being swept along with the crowd.
* By keeping lines of communication open with people—saying 'Good morning' and showing genuine interest in their lives.
* By private prayer, and by offering to pray for the problems of others.
* By keeping our own eyes firmly fixed on Jesus, so that we feel *his* compassion for those around us, and can then begin to share and express it.

The accountable worker is a man for justice

Doing what is right and just and fair (Proverbs 1:3, NIV).

Minor injustices and irritations are very common in places of work. Recently, some men were working in our house, and as we got talking one of them said, 'Do you know, Jim, we've only been offered a three per cent pay rise this year. I mean to say, what use is three per cent! Of course we're not taking it. We're sticking out for something better!'

I expect most working men reading this could recount similar stories. Pay, working conditions and working practice give rise to a lot of friction. Where should we stand as Christian men? Certainly not above the battles, as if they were no concern of ours. If we're committed to our work, believing that it is the place of God's choice for us, then we're committed to justice for all in our place of work, because only justice for all will help capture our place for Christ. Once we stand for justice, we're standing with God who has a deep desire for justice and fairness. Again and again we read in the Bible that he cares greatly about poor widows, orphans, strangers, the oppressed, the badly treated, and those who can't speak for themselves. Perhaps we have to be prepared to go even further and say that we're for justice for others, even if we don't get a fair deal ourselves. Maybe we've got to have our views of justice changed. When we don't agree to some practice at work because it's unfair to a minority, we're just as much standing for God's justice as the Christians who fight for civil rights in oppressed countries. It's the same desire for justice and fairness, stimulated by the same God in both cases, although one case looks more obvious than the other.

So what can we do?

1. We must stand for justice, even though this will inevitably involve us in conflict. Are you prepared for

this, whatever level you work at?

2. Standing for justice will involve some hard thinking. In my experience of industry, not all issues can be easily resolved into right and wrong. A lot of hard thinking and heart searching has to take place—are you prepared to do this?

3. Standing for justice inevitably involves some compromise. Do you know where you can and cannot compromise as a Christian man?

4. Standing for justice will involve some hard and long praying, either by you alone, or with a group. Are you prepared for this?

5. Standing for justice could result in you losing some of your rights. Are you prepared to go without, in order that others might have a little more?

6. Standing for justice might lead you into being more involved with union or management politics and negotiation. Are you prepared for this?

An accountable worker is a man involved

> [Jesus] had to become like his brothers in every way (Hebrews 2:17).

The climax of Christ's life on earth was his death and resurrection, but he didn't treat the rest of his life as secondary in any way. He used the whole of his earthly experience to teach and help us—he was totally committed to the whole of his life here on earth. He expects us to have the same commitment to our own lives here on earth, and as paid work is a major part of that life, then he expects our total commitment to it, as far as is right and possible.

Are you seen to be committed to your place of paid work? Do you support the social club, the union functions, the management parties, retirement parties, leaving meetings, etc? You may be involved at works level if your place of work is small, or at shift or section level if it is large, but unless you are seen to care, within the limits of your other commitments, what hope is there of making significant change for the sake of Christ. His involvement with us was total, and we need to carry something of that involvement into our work place.

The accountable worker is a man for eternity

> Store up riches for yourselves in heaven...for your heart will always be where your riches are (Matthew 6:20–21).

Christian paid workers must never lose sight of the eternal in their daily work. We are there to help those around us become aware of Christ's presence, and ultimately to find him for themselves. This doesn't happen in five minutes, or even five years, and we don't always see the results of our service for Christ. But at all times we are representatives of the King, reminding others by our lives of his claims. In your place of work do you:

1. Represent Christ by your behaviour?
2. Do you try to build bridges with those who are outside of his kingdom? Who are you trying to do this with at the moment?
3. Do you pray for individuals at work to find Christ? Who are you praying for at the moment?
4. Do you invite people to events where they will hear about Christ? Are you on the lookout for events that you can invite people to, and the people to invite to them?
5. Do you try to share your faith, either one-to-one,

or by lending books, tapes, videos and so on? Have you got your personal story about Jesus into a form that is easy for a non-Christian man to listen to during a few quiet minutes? Have you ever thought of inviting someone to work at lunchtime, who can talk about Jesus with your friends?

The accountable worker can succeed—or not

> Be concerned above everything else with the Kingdom of God and with what he requires of you, and he will provide you with all these other things (Matthew 6:33).

There can be no doubt that from a human point of view, Jesus and his mission look to be a disaster. He didn't seem to be able to keep clear of trouble with the authorities, he picked a bunch of useless people to be his closest advisers and friends, he wouldn't seize power when he had the chance, and was finally trapped and killed because the opposition were able to control the courts and manipulate highly placed officials. From a human, success-orientated viewpoint, this was a total failure. From God's point of view, however, it was an unparalleled victory, changing history in an irreversible way. The foundation for this victory was not success or failure, but obedience. Christ kept his eyes fixed on God and his plans and purposes.

In the factory where I worked, we were always talking about 'the competition'—other factories that made the same products as us. But the competition wasn't just with other factories, it was with each other as we tried to succeed in our jobs. The leader of our section was a good man, but we looked on him with something like pity because he couldn't get any further promotion in the factory—he wasn't good enough. He was stuck and we saw him as a failure. Failure is the price paid for living in a success-orientated environment, and it hurts.

I remember how I felt when I didn't get a particular job I wanted. I felt rejected, and I was afraid to tell my work friends in case they started to look at me with pity. It was years before I could really face my feelings.

Have you ever felt this? The success/failure trap is a deadly one, but Christ has delivered us from it. His own life shows us that as it was obedience to his Father that controlled his life and actions, so it must be with us if we are to avoid the success/failure trap. We are working to a different code—we make it our aim to please him. So if success comes, then we give the credit and glory to him, and if disaster comes, we look to him for strength. Are you tempted by success? Are you afraid of failure at work? Christ only asks obedience of us. Are you obedient? If you are, then you can be content no matter what happens. Pray for those you know at work who are caught in the success/failure trap.

The accountable worker never forgets his home

Most men take their work home with them. We may not carry it in our briefcases, but it's a part of us and can't be left behind.

There is a balance between sharing our work with our wife and family, and allowing work to spoil or damage our home life. Do you try to exclude work from your home? Does this help your wife? What does it say to her about your work? Has too much of your work intruded into your home? Does this in any way damage your marriage?

No paid work

Men in the no-paid work situation may have been forced to give up their paid work, either because they have been made redundant, their place of work has closed, or illness has forced them into early retirement. Their finance comes from the state, from savings, or from the jobs that their wives do. No paid work has become very common in the western world, and brings with it a number of problems which seem to be common to all men, whatever their previous level of paid work and responsibility, or their beliefs. Christian men may have spiritual resources to face the no-paid-work situation, but they still have to experience the common problems which present themselves in the following ways:

a) Having no paid work is a tremendous challenge to our self-esteem as men. Recently a lady came up to me and said, 'My husband has been asked to take early retirement at work because of ill health. I think it will do him good. He can rest more and we can have more time together. But he's really upset at the suggestion, and I can't for the life of me understand why.' I had to explain to her that her husband didn't see this as an opportunity, but felt that he was being told that he was no longer capable of holding down his job. For us to feel unwanted at work is a tremendous blow—to our pride, our esteem, our sense of masculinity and our desires to be the breadwinner. Coming to terms with this is very hard, because paid work is seen as the sign of virility and ability, and to be denied work is to be denied the chance to show our masculine strengths. This is the price we pay for equating 'employment' with paid work, rather than seeing paid work as only one means of employing our time.

b) A man with no paid work worries about finances. He gets his state payments and possibly some redundancy money, but this is a poor substitute for a regular salary or pay packet, and it's often a much smaller sum than could be earned. To be short of money in our consumer society is a worry in itself—but how many of us really care about this problem until it's forced on us personally?

c) A man with no paid work faces a social stigma which is very deep rooted. The implication is that he is without paid work because he is idle, or lazy, or wants to live on the state security payments. Despite the enormous number of men without paid work—ordinary, honest, industrious men—this attitude still lingers on.

d) A man with no paid work has too much time. Paid work provides a framework for our lives, giving us a timetable for our days, and providing a feeling of security. Once that structure goes, and there's time for everything, the large amount of unstructured time becomes a real problem.

e) A man with no paid work has a lot of time for his wife and children. This is a good thing if the marriage is stable, but if it isn't then there's so much more time for the problems to come to the surface, and so much more time to dwell on them.

f) A man with no paid work loses touch with his friends. Paid work provides a social circle for men, and once the work has gone so does this daily contact with like-minded men, doing like-minded things in a familiar routine and atmosphere.

g) A man with no paid work loses hope. He has been taught throughout his education that he can and will have a job. It's part of his expectation, and the means of achieving his material dreams. When the paid work goes, there often isn't much left to hope for, or to look forward to. This is the real danger with words like 'employment' and 'unemployment'. They polarize life and leave no room for anything else. 'Paid work' and 'no paid work', even though they are unusual terms, do leave room for other goals in life, and there can be so much more to life than just paid work.

The Christian man with no paid work

Many Christian men are in the no-paid-work situation. What does God expect of them so that not only do they live according to his pattern, but they also show to others that there is a biblical way of approaching this experience?

We recognize that there is no easy option

> Jesus said 'If anyone would come after me, he must deny himself and take up his cross and follow me (Mark 8:34, NIV).

Christian and non-Christian men both suffer when they have no paid work. In fact sometimes Christian men have an even rougher time because they have unreal expectations of what God will do for them.

One Christian man explained the problem that this caused for him: 'When I was made redundant, I was sure that the Lord had a job for me, so I prayed and relaxed. That was a year ago. I still haven't got a job, and some of my non-believing friends have. I find this hard to understand.'

This sort of story is quite common, and reminds us

again that being a Christian man doesn't give us any easy solutions to the problems that face us. We have to learn to accept the hardness of life, and to be willing to take up our cross and follow Christ. If we can do this, not only do we stay close to God, but we earn the right to help others who are in the same position and who do not know God. If they see us struggling like them, but having different resources, then it's possible they will start to enquire about the things of God.

Are you looking for the easy way out? Are you expecting God to remove your difficulties overnight? Will you go on struggling through the problems of not having paid work for Christ's sake, looking for his purpose in it? Will you let Christ use your situation to help others in the same position?

We know that God is in charge of our lives

> We know that in all things God works for good with those who love him, those whom he has called according to his purpose (Romans 8:28).

When Philip died, I struggled with the grief for many years, and I often felt like giving up on God because things didn't seem to be getting any better. I simply couldn't see how he was helping me. But he never gave up on me, and I have slowly come to understand that when he says 'all things work for good', he really means all things. Now that the darkness is beginning to clear, I am able to see the truth of these words and of God's faithfulness to me.

This same conviction can be found in the heart of every Christian man. No matter how bad things get, we know that God is in charge of our lives. It's not false optimism based on vague feelings, but clear biblical truth based on experience. It's a conviction that holds true in the no-paid-work experience, as in any of the experiences of our lives. Men that don't know Christ must build on other things—the hope that something will turn up, resignation to the situation, pointless time fillers—and our job is to help them find the real certainty of our faith. If we have it, then it will show and others will see it. Is your knowledge of God being in charge a help to others today?

And even though paid work has ceased for us, that gives us more time to work on those areas of our lives which never cease—our position as servant husband, loving father and caring son. Perhaps God is giving you the opportunity to develop these areas. Are you prepared to see it like this?

We have a great potential to achieve

> I keep striving to win the prize for which Christ Jesus has already won me to himself (Philippians 3:12).

St Paul, who wrote this verse, had a very clear experience of surrendering his life to Jesus. But that was only the start of his adventures. From that beginning, he went on to preach about Jesus all over the ancient world. He just kept moving forward in his faith and experience until he died. We have surrendered to the same God, and face the same challenge—to keep moving forward in our experience until we die. This is the great challenge and thrill of our faith.

This opportunity of growth, and of reaching our potential, is open to Christian men who have no paid work in a very special way. We can give most of our time to Christ—become workers for him in our homes, street, church, club and community. The time and the income are provided—all that's needed is the vision and the desire.

As you consider your position as an unpaid worker, these questions might help you begin to see things more clearly:

a) Is God's purpose for your life at this moment paid work? It might have been in the past and it might be in the future, but what is his purpose at this moment?

b) There are people that perhaps only you can help—the millions of other unpaid workers, many of whom have no faith in Christ and for whom the future looks very uncertain. You're in the same position—perhaps you can help a few of them. Will you try?

c) God has given you the chance to make up a brand new timetable for your life. It's a very positive opportunity to start again. Are you taking it?

d) You've now got more time to serve God in many ways. Are you looking for the opportunities?

We need the help of others

Help to carry one another's burdens... (Galatians 6:2).

If the unpaid Christian man is going to survive the stresses and strains of his life, and use the opportunities they present, he is going to need help. In fact, God expects us to share our struggles with others, and if we don't, we're being disobedient.

So where are we to look for support? The first person must be our wife. It is of the utmost importance to share with her how we are feeling and what we're trying to achieve. Do you treat your wife as your friend and adviser?

We also need a man that we can meet with regularly,

to share our masculine worries and fears. Have you got such a friend?

Our church can also provide a place of friendship and support—does it help you in this way?

A MAN AND LEISURE TIME

I once played squash with a friend who was a monk. We arrived at the changing rooms and his habit caused quite a stir! After our game we returned to the changing rooms, where we met a different set of men to the ones we had met on the way in. They were laughing and smoking, and the language was very masculine! Imagine their complete shock when my friend put on his monk's habit, complete with sandals and cross! The language suddenly became very refined, cigarettes were instantly put out, and everyone began discussing the weather with deep concern.

Despite what we wear, or how we behave, we don't stop being Christian men because we're at rest. The opposite is true because when we relax, others can see more clearly what we are really like. So it's vitally important that we are as much God's men when at rest as when we're at work or non-paid work. What does he expect of us?

Relaxing—part of God's plan

> The apostles gathered round Jesus and reported to him all they had done and taught. Then, because so many people were coming and going that they did not even have a chance to eat, he said to them, 'Come with me by yourselves to a quiet place and get some rest' (Mark 6:30–31, NIV).

Rest and relaxation is part of God's divine plan for our lives. He stated this clearly in the Old Testament, and Jesus insisted that his followers put it into practice in his day. Any man that doesn't take rest seriously is a fool.

I can still remember one man very well. He had opened a new business and he worked at it every day of the week. From early in the morning till late at night he worked, and his business prospered. Unfortunately he didn't, and he died of a heart attack after six months.

Some men say that they're too busy to take rest or holidays, but a Christian man can never say this. He knows that this attitude is outside of God's plan for us. Rest and relaxation are not a luxury. Do you relax? Do you take leisure time as part of your obedience to Christ? Do you ever think that you *must* work because of the demands of your job? Have you perhaps got an overexaggerated view of your usefulness?

Relaxing—do not be uncritical

> We make it our goal to please him (2 Corinthians 5:9, NIV).

We are answerable to Christ for all we do, and it's our desire and hope to please him in every part of our lives. So when we're considering our leisure time, it's important that what we do is in line with his will. There are some questions which we need to ask about our rest, to ensure that it pleases Jesus:

a) Does it make me more relaxed and better able to serve Christ?

b) Does it take me away from my wife and family

too much? Does it stretch my resources too far? (Some hobbies and relaxations are very expensive and can be a drain on family resources.)

c) Do my relaxations identify me with things I should not be identified with? Can a Christian man be involved in an activity sponsored by a tobacco firm? Can a Christian man be involved in a hobby which is excessively violent—like boxing or karate?

d) Do the things I relax with cause others to stumble? Do they say, 'Well, if Jim does it then it must be OK. So I'll do it as well.'

Within the boundaries of these questions, there are many enjoyable things we can do to relax. What do you do?

Leisure is simple evangelism

> Go and make disciples of all nations (Matthew 28:19, NIV).

Many Christians find it difficult to get involved in making disciples, even though they know Christ commands it. Leisure time activities give us a simple opportunity to get involved in the discipleship process, and have a good time as well. Through our rest time activities, we come into contact with people whom we might otherwise never get to know. Building up these friendships is so natural in a relaxed environment where there is a shared common interest, and eventually these friendships can be used to interest people in the things of God. Being involved in the gardening club, the squash league, or the community service programme where we get alongside non-believing men, is as much part of evangelism as a parish outreach or a big crusade.

Your leisure activities are God's front line. Do you see them as such? If you do, then enjoy yourself and build bridges of friendship for the kingdom.

A MAN AND THE CHURCH

> All of you are Christ's body, and each one is a part of it (1 Corinthians 12:27).

For the man who has surrendered his life to Christ, involvement in a local church or fellowship is an essential part of his daily life, not an optional extra. God's principles are quite clear and if we're ever tempted to believe that we can be a Christian outside of a local fellowship, or if anyone else claims that it is possible, we only need to refer them to what God says:

a) [Christ] is the head of his body, the church' (Colossians 1:18).

Christ has placed himself at the head of those who believe in him. We are so important to him that he will not let anyone else assume this vital position. If the church is that important to him, then we can have no excuse for adopting a casual approach to our membership of it. Anyone who says: 'I can be a Christian without going to church,' is saying in effect, 'Christ may see the church as important, but I don't!' It is impossible for a Christian man to say such a thing.

Have you ever been tempted to see membership of your local fellowship as optional?

b) Christ loved the church, and gave his life for it (Ephesians 5:25).

Christ's commitment to the church is total—he gave his life for it. We're expected to have the same deep and total commitment to our fellowship.

Do you love your fellow believers so much that you would give your life for them?

c) Each one of us has received a special gift . . . He did this to prepare all God's people for the work of Christian service, in order to build up the body of Christ (Ephesians 4:7, 12).

The church is where God has deposited all the gifts necessary for us to grow as believers. No individual has all the gifts, but collectively we have everything we need. No man can afford therefore to neglect being a member of the church, for he needs the gifts and skills of other believers so that he and they can reach full potential.

What can you give? What do you receive?

These are the principles on which the Christian man belongs to the church. The benefits of belonging are very great, for us and our families, and can be summed up in the following ways.

We experience personal growth and development

> We must grow up in every way to Christ, who is the head (Ephesians 4:15).

A man came to Christ five years ago. He had no previous experience of church attendance, but joined a small fellowship. Over those five years he has grown enormously, and he himself admits: 'When I started coming to church, I never imagined that one day I would be preaching once a month! In fact, if you had even suggested it, I would have laughed. But that is what has happened over five years. The opportunities to speak have come, and I've discovered that Christ has given me the ability to do it. Bit by bit I'm getting more effective.'

We're not all called to be preachers, but through our fellowship we will experience steady growth in ability, confidence and skill, as week by week we worship and learn. The growing experiences don't just come on a Sunday, but in many other ways:

* Through belonging to a smaller group, like a men's fellowship, or a home-based discussion group.
* Through times of prayer with one or two others on a regular basis.
* Through the events of our daily lives, which others are able to help us understand.
* Through social activities and time spent together.

Are you making the most of the growth opportunities that your local fellowship can provide? The following questions might help you to know. Answer them in the light of the last six months.

* How has your experience of Christ changed in the last six months?
* How are you getting on as a husband and father?
* Are you gaining a deeper understanding of the Bible?

* Can you see God at work in your life more clearly now?
* Are you gaining a better understanding of the social issues which face you?
* Do you have more compassion for the world?
* Are you getting to know the men of your church better?
* Are you getting the most out of the teaching provided by your fellowship—by taking notes, making tapes, reading books, and so on?
* Do you meet regularly for prayer with someone else?
* Do you go to a small group, and are you giving and getting the best from it?
* Does your men's fellowship group meet your needs?

If you haven't grown as you would have liked, perhaps you've got to ask some questions—either about your personal involvement with your church, or about the programmes your local church is offering you.

We learn to relate faith to everyday life

> I am sure that God, who began this good work in you, will carry it on until it is finished on the Day of Christ Jesus (Philippians 1:6).

We all have to live in the real world, however much we like being with the members of our fellowship. For many of us this means being a lone Christian in an office or factory, a street, or a club. Faced with this kind of isolation, it can sometimes be very hard to understand what the issues are, and how we can relate them to our faith. Others before us have abandoned the faith in the face of the pressures of the world. One of St Paul's close friends gave up: 'Demas fell in love with this present world and has deserted me, going off to Thessalonica' (2 Timothy 4:9).

The same could easily happen to us, and it's within our church fellowship that we can prevent this happening, and sort out the issues—working out how they will affect our lives. Not only do we get the advice and help of others, but at the same time we can give them our advice and help. It's very definitely two-way traffic.

Here are just a few issues that a Christian man has to sort out. They're fairly hard, and there are many others like them. What does your faith say about these questions? You might find it useful to form a small group of committed men, and tackle these together. This could be a way of getting men together in your church. Remember you are trying to see how a Christian man will respond in these situations.

* How does the teaching of the Bible relate to twentieth-century industrial and commercial practice?
* How does the teaching of the Bible relate to twentieth-century social standards?
* Do the promises of the Bible hold true when everything is going wrong and prayers don't seem to be getting answered?
* Am I entitled to buy a video when two thirds of the world are starving?
* How can I go on believing in a loving God in the face of so much injustice and so many disasters?

* Am I allowed to cheat at work—use phones, etc? Do I work hard for my employer? Am I fair to my employees? Does God care about me because I have no paid work?
* Do I treat my wife fairly? How does my faith help me through infidelity, separation and divorce?
* Do I treat my children fairly—what if they get into trouble? How does my faith help me to cope?

We are helped to share our faith

> Be ready at all times to answer anyone who asks you to explain the hope you have in you, but do it with gentleness and respect (1 Peter 3:15–16).

If we are going to capture our places of work and leisure for Christ, then we are going to have to get involved in sharing our faith. Many Christians get alarmed at the thought of evangelism, imagining that it will involve them standing on street corners preaching! If God leads you that way it might, but there's so much more to evangelism than preaching or leading a person in a prayer of response to Christ, and as we look at the whole process, perhaps you will be able to find a part that you can play in it.

Evangelism is a sequence of events. People move through this sequence until they surrender to Christ and serve him for the rest of their lives. We can evangelize people entirely on our own, but if we do we must realize this isn't how God planned that it should happen. God planned that we should reach out *together*. I've always felt more at ease when I share my faith knowing there is an active fellowship behind me.

There will be occasions when I'm on my own, but I believe these are the exception, rather than the rule. When Jesus sent his disciples out on an evangelistic mission, he sent them out in pairs, and when he left his final commission, he left it not to one but to a group of men. God understands our need for support and I believe that we should be looking for an evangelistic strategy emerging from the heart of our local fellowship and returning to it. This way, we have the support we need, and so will those we are reaching.

Have you been trying to go it alone at work? Will your local fellowship give you more support? They'll never know you need it unless you tell them.

Has your local fellowship a strategy for reaching out with the Good News? If not, perhaps you should start asking questions. I've written extensively about a strategy for reaching men in my book *Manhunt*.

So, what exactly *is* evangelism, and how can we fit in?

The desire to reach others with the Good News

This has its origin in the heart of *God*, not the heart of man. Jesus has a heart of compassion for lost men and women, seeing them as 'sheep without a shepherd' (Matthew 9:36).

So, the desire to reach others starts with a willingness to spend more time with God, being changed by him and being filled with his compassion. Have you been looking anywhere other than to Christ for your motivation? Spend a little more time with him, so that you have his vision in your heart.

Evangelism is rooted in prayer

My job is a very public one. I'm always on public

platforms and pulpits preaching about Jesus, but I've long since learnt that the real action is with those who pray.

Recently I was preaching in a church, and a small group had met to pray through the sermon in the room behind the pulpit. As I preached, I could hear their prayers through the wall and this greatly inspired me. When I had finished, many responded to my appeal to accept Jesus as Lord. At an appropriate moment, I slipped into the prayer room, and one of the pray-ers went to the door. 'Praise God,' he cried. 'Esmie has come forward, and Mike and Peter!' Each time he mentioned a name, the whole room seemed to sigh with joy. Another of the pray-ers said to me, 'Jim, we've prayed for each one of those people tonight with great intensity, and the Lord has answered each prayer.'

Prayer is where the action is, as God hears and answers in his time and in his way. Are you praying for people to come to know Christ? I don't mean a general prayer, but prayers for specific people? God will honour your prayers, although you won't always see the answers. Will you start praying now? If you will, then you're in the heart of evangelism.

Build bridges

Recently, I spoke about Jesus at a school, and I used as simple language as I could. At the end of my talk I asked for questions, and I was asked: 'Sir, is God a spaceman?' 'Sir, how can you speak to a cloud?' 'Sir, what's "saved" mean?' I suddenly realized how far away from me these kids were, even though I thought I had spoken in a language they could understand. This can be true of many of those who don't know

Christ. They can be a long way from the kingdom, and need us to be very patient and understanding as they begin to think their way towards Christ. But how will they ever do that if we Christian men stay in our fellowships, with our Christian friends, doing Christian things? We need to build bridges with the non-Christian world so that those who don't know Christ can cross them, and through us get to know him. How can we do it?

Form friendships with those who don't know Christ. Of course they have to be genuine friendships, not just for the purpose of evangelism. This takes time and effort. Who do you have as a friend who doesn't yet know Christ? Is there someone in your street, work place or club whom you could befriend, in the hope that eventually you can help them find Christ?

Invite them to fellowship events. By bringing men to our fellowship events, we help them to begin to meet other men who are believers, and hopefully their minds begin to open.

Bob had no interest at all in Christian things until he moved into a new area and his wife started attending church. He went along occasionally, and for the first time in his life came into contact with men who were both ordinary—in his eyes—and also committed Christians. After a while, he admitted: 'I'd never thought there was anything in this Christianity before. But now I've met Tim and Pete and Dave, and now I'm thinking that if they believe, then there might be something in it after all.'

Events don't have to be spiritual. Why not have a sports night, or a video, or a darts match? It's the contact with others that is important. Does your fellowship have invitable events for men? If not, isn't it time to start having some?

Invite them to spiritual events. But make sure they are good ones and that the speaker, if there is one, is a man's man. This sort of process takes time, but with the prayer back-up you might be surprised at the openness of people that you thought were not interested. Man is a spiritual animal and we have a spiritual truth to share, so don't be afraid to invite people to hear about spiritual things.

Share your faith with them. Given the opportunity, many of us can share the story of how we came to know Christ. Maybe you think you can't, but you can with the right preparation. Try this method:

* Write out the story of how you came to know Christ. Include what you were like before you came to know him, how you came to know him, and what things have changed since. (If you don't have a 'before I came to Christ' section, because you seem to have known Christ from a very early age, or because coming to him was a gradual experience, then concentrate on what he means to you today.) Include at least *one* example from recent months of how Jesus has helped you.
* Leave this for a few days, and then come back to it. Anything need changing?
* Rewrite, and read it to a Christian friend. Ask for his comments and make alterations if necessary.
* Underline the main points and commit them to memory.
* Ask God for a chance to share your story.

Some can go much further and share the whole gospel

story, either from memory or using a booklet to explain the gospel. There's nothing inferior about using a booklet and going through it with someone. It has the great advantage that you can leave the booklet with them afterwards. Do you carry a supply of suitable booklets to share from, or give away? Are you able to give an account of your faith? Is it time to work on your story to make it usable?

This is obviously a very brief look at evangelism in action. For a longer look, see my book *Time to Share*. One thing is certain, as a Christian man you have the responsibility to be involved somewhere in this process. But it is a very broad process, and there's need for people at every level of involvement. Where do you fit in?

There are other things you can do as a Christian man with a desire to reach others. How about the possibility of:

a) A Prayer and Fellowship cell at work, or with your friends that are in a non-paid-work situation? It doesn't take much organizing, and it could be the beginning of much Christian influence.

b) A Christian Union, again in a work or non-work situation. This is a little more ambitious than a prayer cell, as you invite speakers in and reach out through specific events. There are Christian Unions or fellowships in many branches of industry, schools, medicine and social services. Perhaps there's already one near you, or if not, why not think of starting something. Christian Union leaders and members must build links with local fellowships, as well as with Christian friends at work or wherever they operate. Many Christian groups die because they get no support from a fellowship outside their situation. Sometimes this happens because no one knows of their existence! If you're really stumped for ideas about how to begin, the Evangelical Alliance will be able to help you. (Their address is: 186 Kennington Park Road, London SE11 4BT.)

We learn what it means to disciple

> If anyone wants to come with me...he must forget self, carry his cross, and follow me (Mark 8:34).

Surrendering to Christ is the beginning of our experience. We then have to learn what it means to follow him—to be his disciples. Our fellowship helps us to disciple and be disciples in these ways:

Caring for new believers

Evangelism does not stop at the moment of surrender. Our responsibility is to see that new believers are cared for—this is the beginning of discipleship and it can be done both on a one-to-one basis, and in small groups. The areas that have to be covered are:

* Understanding the facts of Jesus.
* Relating new faith to everyday life.
* Understanding about prayer, the Bible and worship.
* Coping with challenges of the world.
* Coping with pressures of friends.
* Finding areas of service.
* Helping other members of the family appreciate what has happened.

The very best way to learn this sort of thing is for someone else to show it to us. This would mean meeting with someone else on a regular basis and sharing experiences. It would mean making sure that our Christian life is up to the mark—we can't teach others if we're not right ourselves. Is there someone that you can help in this way, at church or at work? It's as we learn from others, and learn to depend on each other, that we become disciples.

Discipled yourself

It isn't enough to try and offer discipleship to others—who is discipling you? Who do you talk things over with, and whose experience do you depend on to help you? If you want to meet regularly in this way with someone else, it doesn't have to be too formal—it could take place during a walk, or over a drink. But we all need someone to help us.

Discipling your family

As the head of your household, you have a special discipleship position with respect to your wife and children. If they are not getting discipled, then it's for you to do something about it.

* Does your wife have someone she can go and talk things over with? If not, why not, and what are you doing about it?

* Do your children have a friend and adviser, apart from you? Or are they getting the help they need through the fellowship teaching programme? You will only know the answer to this if you take an active interest in what is going on in the fellowship youth programme. Do you take an interest?

* Can your family relate their faith to their everyday life? How can you help here?
* Are they growing in understanding? If not, what can you do about it?

Disciples become leaders

As we grow as Christian men, some of us can move into leadership positions within our fellowships—and there is a great need for leaders at *every* level:

* Leaders of worship and spiritual oversight.
* Leaders of pastoral care.
* Leaders of small home-based groups.
* Leaders of social activity in the church and the community.
* Leaders of practical work.
* Leaders of administration.
* Leaders of youth work and other special areas.
* Leaders for prayer.

These are just a few of the needs of your fellowship, and even if you're not called to be *the* leader, you could be a co-leader, or an assistant leader.

What are the leadership needs of your church? Do you even know? Are you prepared to volunteer, or at least talk over the possibilities with your full-time pastor? There are many needs and it's possible that they are not all being met because you're the one to fill them.

Disciples suffer

This is part of the discipleship role—it's the taking up of the cross to follow Christ. It happened to him, and it will happen to us. Those we are trying to disciple and lead will often hurt us and it's easy to wonder at times whether it's all worth it. But this *is* the price—will you pay it?

Disciples attract other men

What I have written in this section has been for Christian men. If you're not a church-going man, I hope that it has given you an insight into what you can expect if you surrender to Christ and become a member of a local church fellowship. The life of a disciple is a tough one, but it is also an exciting and attractive one, and it attracts other men. They know that there is something different in us, something which is testing us but at the same time fulfilling us in a way that nothing in their experience has ever managed to do. If you're living the discipled life, then you're like a light set on top of a hill, and many will find Christ because of you. Spend a few minutes now thanking him for this privilege and praying for those around you who do not yet know Christ.

5

A Man on His Own

This book is being written by a married man and will be read by many men who are also married. However, there is a section of our society which is not married—single men, divorced men and widowed men, and being a Christian man has implications for these states as well. I want to look at these now.

THE SINGLE MAN

> I have learned the secret of being content in any and every situation (Philippians 4:12, NIV).

Young men in their late teens and very early twenties tend not to be particularly worried about being single. Society doesn't see this as unusual—after all, these men will probably get married very soon because these are the marrying years. But as the years go by, and marriage doesn't come, the pressures start to build up, both from within and without. Society begins to look oddly at such men. Why can't they find a wife? Are they homosexual, or have they got other problems which they are keeping hidden? For a single man himself, there are many questions to be faced, and difficulties to surmount. We live in a 'marrying' society, so being single is bound to generate problems.

Here are some of the problems which a single man, Christian or otherwise, has to face. This list may be of help to those men who are married and have single male friends. If you have a good enough relationship with a single man, you might find it helpful to talk it through with them.

* A man might be single and not want to be. What does he do? It isn't always easy to handle relationships with women when this is in the back of his mind.

* A man can be single and want female company. How does he get this without appearing to want more? As time goes by, the ability to just converse with a woman begins to get more difficult.

* A man can be single, but the pressure of his sexuality is as strong as that of a married man. How does he cope?

* A single man always comes home to an empty house or flat. The clothes he threw on the floor before he went out are still in exactly the same place when he comes home. He wants to talk, to share his day, but there's no one there, and there's no one there in the middle of the night either.

* Being single in a married world limits the social circle considerably. Events are geared towards couples and families, and single men can easily feel left out. If a single man wants to go out, he has to go

on his own, or make arrangements with other single people to go and this can be tedious and wearing.

There is a positive side to singleness. It provides possibilities which are not always there for a married man. For example:

* A single man can be single and very happy about it. He may not wish to marry, preferring the single life, or he may have come to terms with singleness. It's easy for married men to forget this side of singleness. Being single is a respectable position, and if a man is single and happy then society has no right to ask unnecessary questions.

* A single man has time flexibility. He hasn't got to 'get home for the kids' and so there are more possibilities open to him.

* A single man has time to develop skills and hobbies, time to read and think, time for culture.

* Being single gives job flexibility. A single man can move to a new job much more easily than a married man who has to consider his wife and children.

* Being single has financial flexibility. A married man has so many claims on his financial resources, and many of them recurring. A single man may have more resources at his sole command to do what he likes with.

* A single man has flexibility in his friendships. He can travel to friends and keep his relationships going in a way that is difficult for married men.

Being single is both a positive and a negative experience. The single Christian man has a different perspective on his singleness, which helps him to get more from the benefits and to cope better with the strains.

The Christian single man

He builds on the facts

The Bible offers us three facts of singleness for our encouragement:

a) Singleness is *not* failure: 'It is good for a man not to marry' (1 Corinthians 7:1, NIV). There's nothing wrong with being single—whatever society says or thinks of us. It's an honourable position to hold and the Bible encourages us in this belief.

There's nothing wrong with wanting to be married either, and this desire needs to be brought to God, with the willingness to accept 'no' or 'not yet' from him. God's guidance seems to be that in whatever state we find ourselves, we must believe this is his plan and purpose for us at this point in our lives.

Do you sometimes believe that your singleness is a sign of your failure to get on with women? Do you feel the pressure of society on you? Spend some time reminding yourself that you are chosen and precious to God. Thank him for the situation you are in, and ask him to make his plans clear to you in his own time and his own way. If you are single, your married Christian friends need your help and encouragement as much as you need theirs. Marriage is not a bed of roses, as previous pages have made clear. Many marriages might be helped by *your* support.

Spend some time praying for those you know who are married. Ask God to help you be more patient and understanding with your married friends. Ask him to show you what you can do to encourage their marriages, as they try to understand your singleness.

b) Christ understands the pain. 'He was despised and rejected by men, a man of sorrows, and familiar with suffering' (Isaiah 53:3, NIV).

It's quite clear that Christ understands the pain and frustration of being single, just as he understands all the other pains and sorrows of life. He came into our world and took our human form with all its drawbacks. He entered totally into the pain and frustration of singleness—in fact, being single himself, he understands better than anyone what you sometimes feel and experience. Can you spend some time bringing all your frustrations to him now? Your desire for female company, for a wife, the emptiness of your heart, your life, your home? I know that this is asking a lot and I know that it will take a lot of courage. Perhaps if you can honestly share it with Christ, then he will make someone available that can also listen with sympathy and understanding.

c) Christ creates opportunities: '"Come follow me" Jesus said, "and I will make you fishers of men"' (Mark 1:17, NIV).

Being single gives you unique opportunities to grow into maturity as a Christian, and to be involved in creative Christian service. There are some jobs in God's service which can only be done by single men. There are some things that God can only teach us as single men, and there are some jobs in his service which are going to need *all* of our creative drive and ability, and God knows that we won't have the extra for a wife too. These are possibilities that need to be considered. Are you asking God to give you a partner when he's really saying, 'I need a brave and dedicated single man—will you serve me in this capacity?'

You have a lot to offer him. For example:

* You can offer him your home, room or flat. It may be empty, but that's an opportunity for God to use it. Perhaps there are people who would long to get away somewhere for a day, or a night? Perhaps your fellowship wants a room to use for a meeting? Perhaps it could become a drop-in centre for people. It's a question of seeing the potential, isn't it?

* You can offer him your flexibility—of time, money, house or job. Who knows what God might do with any or all of these? Many people are in need, and perhaps you have the time and money to help. Again, it's a question of seeing the vision and acting on it.

* You can offer him your abilities. Perhaps God wants you to train, or learn, or prepare for needs that will come in your fellowship. Many pastors are not good administrators—so maybe you've got to acquire the skills and offer them to him. Maybe your fellowship needs a computer and someone who can operate it. Can you acquire the necessary skills and do the job? Most organizations need voluntary drivers. Can you offer time? There's so much you can learn. Will you ask God for the training opportunities?

* Think of your married friends again. Who does their decorating, mends their fences, does their shopping? You might be able to help in these ways. We've a large family and there's always so much to do. We're glad of any help, and there are millions like us. Can you help?

He knows that God has a long-term view

> Many are the plans in a man's heart, but it is the Lord's purpose that prevails (Proverbs 19:21, NIV).

The Christian single man can have complete confidence in the long-term planning and perspective of his God. A twenty-five-year-old man need not worry about being thirty-five and single, because God knows all about his thirty-fifth year, and his hundredth year come to that, because God is in control. A non-Christian man is denied this confidence, and is forced back on his own resources. He might change his image, change his behaviour and lifestyle, and relax his morals to change his state.

A Christian single man said recently: 'If I were not a Christian, I would change my ways and go out and find a wife at any price, but because I'm a Christian, I basically believe that God does have a plan for my life, and so I hang on in faith. I would like to be married, but it's not to be for the moment. So in my life I try to glorify God and enjoy him for ever. He knows what the future holds.'

Spend a few moments thinking back over the years of your life. Can you see God's hand at work? Now imagine the years ahead, and trust in faith that God will work in these years as well. Sometimes we concentrate so much on the present, that we forget the greatness of God and his very long-term view. Do you make this mistake? The story of Abraham is a very encouraging one for those who have forgotten the long-term purposes of God (Genesis 12–22).

He has a family

> The group of believers was one in mind and heart (Acts 4:32).

Single Christian men do belong to a family—the earthly church family of Christ's people. Sadly, so many churches take little apparent notice of their single members. We've become a place for families, and this only makes it worse for the single men. However, in a fellowship which recognizes the need, a single man can find a real home and real love. If your fellowship doesn't have an understanding of single people's needs, then perhaps it's your job to help them come to an understanding. And if you're married, is it time you started to find out what they would welcome—and that includes both men and women. Most important of all, do you as a married couple open your home to single people, or do you just invite families round? Your home and your love might make a big difference to single people.

He has help with his emotions

> [Jesus] had to become like his brothers in every way... and now he can help those who are tempted, because he himself was tempted and suffered. (Hebrews 2:17–18).

We cannot make rules to govern our emotions. By their very nature they tend to be beyond rules, and often break all social conventions. Children don't worry about this—they howl and scream whenever they feel like it. Adults try to keep things bottled up, but like water, the emotions find another way out. Single men are in a difficult position. Married men can always share things with their wives, and wives are generally very understanding and loving. But what does a single man do when he desires love, support, sympathy and a listening ear?

There is no easy solution here, but there are some possibilities:

* He goes to Christ. The Lord Jesus became like us in every way, so he does understand.
* He goes to a trusted female friend. A married woman can be a great help here, and this underlines again the importance to single people of a married home where they can feel at home.
* He goes to a trusted male friend. The sharing of common masculine problems in an informal atmosphere can often help.
* He looks to his church. If the local fellowship has an awareness of single people and their needs, then this could be a place of help and strength.

The key question has to be asked: are you prepared, as a single man, to share your real emotions with someone else so that they can help and encourage you? Will you, as a single man, be on the look out for other single men who might be glad of your help and encouragement?

THE DIVORCED MAN

> I make all things new (Revelation 21:5).

A large number of men in this country have known the joy and privilege of marriage, but that marriage is now over. These men have come to terms with being single again, and it's a difficult change, with many problems and challenges. Christian and non-Christian alike have to experience these problems. There's no short cut. We're going to look briefly at the problems, and then set against them the Christian alternative. As we do, pray for anyone you know who is divorced.

A divorced man is a grieving man

Facing life after divorce is just like facing the process of grief. There's the shock, the pain of separation, the blankness of the future, and the ever present past to haunt and perplex. Places that had strong associations for the now dead marriage are avoided, and relationships with friends who were joint friends have to be rethought. Life can look extremely empty, and there's a whole process of coming to terms with past, present and future.

Guilt and anger are present

The end of a marriage may appear to be the only creative way forward, but it leaves behind a legacy of anger and guilt. The anger can be directed at the other partner, or anyone or anything else that can be held to be responsible. The guilt is directed internally, and the man whose marriage has broken feels that in some way he is a failure. This guilt and anger stays around for a long time, and it can cloud any new relationships. A new friendship with a woman can often be blighted by the awareness of former things.

Practical things can be a problem

In most marriages, the husband and wife do different tasks—perhaps she irons and he decorates. Now the man has to do everything, and he has to learn these new things while his confidence has taken a battering and he's feeling low, or insecure. Maybe some tasks were shared—perhaps the man and wife decorated together. Now this becomes a single-handed task and consequently more difficult, or more boring. What's more, there are some tasks that seem to be beyond us, yet to ask for help would be to admit to our inadequacies and incompetence, and as men, we're not going to admit those to anyone.

Sexual matters become difficult

We've already looked at length at a man and his sexuality, and I'm not going to cover that ground again. But the divorced man has a particular problem. He once had a regular sexual pattern and now that's gone. In some ways it's easier to live with what you've never had than to go without what you used to have regularly. The temptation to look for casual sex is strong and hard to resist.

Explanations have to be found

A public explanation for the marriage break up has to be found for the benefit of friends and acquaintances, and this often takes the form of face-saving excuses: 'It was all her mother's fault,' or 'We weren't made for each other,' or 'She fancied someone else.' These public explanations enable us to hide our vulnerability and weakness. As men, we don't want anyone to see this side of us. But there's also the need for a private explanation: 'Well, I just didn't give her enough time,' or 'I should have known at the beginning.' Having no private explanation hinders relationships with people in the future.

The divorced man may become a single parent family—or a grieving parent

A husband could find himself with the responsibility of looking after a child, but he's more likely to become a grieving parent with the children going with mother and him granted the right of access. This can be a very unsatisfying arrangement, and a caring man can feel that he has lost his loved ones. Whatever happens, relations with the children are going to be difficult for both parents.

His pride is hurt

We are so sure of ourselves, that to have to face the failure of our marriage is really painful. This is where a Christian man has many resources to help him.

His emotions are in a turmoil

Yet there's no way a man will show them. So he bottles them all up and this begins to affect work and other relationships.

All divorced men suffer—Christian or otherwise. As I've said again and again, being a Christian does not exempt us from the experiences of the rest of humanity. Sometimes, Christian men suffer more because they think God will see them through, and he apparently has not done so. How many Christian men reading this have prayed and prayed for their marriages, still to see them end in ruin?

The older I get, the more I realize that there are no easy solutions to the problems of life. But there is a basis for hope in the Christian position, and the possibility of new beginnings. If you are a Christian man, then make sure that your post-divorce life is built on these foundations. If you're not a Christian man, these are the foundations that Christ can offer you. If you're a married man, use these foundations to help you be more understanding and loving towards your divorced friends.

The Christian man and divorce

A Christian man has a method of facing failure

> When I am weak, then I am strong (2 Corinthians 12:10).

Underneath the divorce experience are so many emotions: the damage to our pride, the shame, the embarrassment, the disappointment, the need for help and comfort, and the sense of failure. As Christians, we are able to come to terms with our inadequacy and failure—because Christ accepts us as we are. When Peter denied knowing Jesus (Mark 14:66–72) and then realized what he had done 'he broke down and cried'. He knew his own emptiness, and unreliability.

Have you wept with despair at the emptiness of your life, and your failure to live up to Christ's standards, and the brokenness of your marriage? The good news for us is that the Christian faith is not a message of failure, but of forgiveness and new beginnings. Far from abandoning Peter because of his failure, Jesus gave him the job of building up the new Christian church. Christ accepts, uses and welcomes failures. Spend a few moments now thinking about this truth. No matter how bad things have been, and how much you are to blame, Christ loves *you* and gave his life for *you*.

This doesn't make failure any less painful. Nor does it excuse us from the responsibility of sorting things out, and that can be very costly to us. But it takes away the sting of the inner hurt and restores our confidence.

* Are you still trapped by a sense of failure and guilt? Bring all these feelings to Jesus now, and ask him to help you sort them out.

* Are your present relationships clouded by the events of the past? Ask God to bring his healing power into your present life.

* Are there people from the days of the divorce that you need to ask forgiveness of, and give your forgiveness to—your former wife, your children, another man? Ask for God's wisdom on these very sensitive matters.

* Spend a few moments thanking God for his forgiveness and his love for you. Ask him to bless your present life.

* Do you have a friend with whom you could share your feelings? Ask God to lead you to someone who will listen to you.

Christ shares our pain

> God made him who had no sin to be sin for us (2 Corinthians 5:21, NIV).

We don't have to explain how we feel to Jesus. He understands because he became like us in every way—even to the point of taking our sin upon himself. When our son Philip died, Christ didn't stand outside the delivery room of the maternity hospital, waiting till it was all over. He came right into the room, stood beside us, and said in effect: 'I understand how you feel—

friends of mine died as well.'

He does the same for you in your divorce, and he does it for your former wife as well. If you are asking the question, 'Why has God let this happen to me?', then I can't give you an answer. But if you are asking, 'Has God abandoned me?', from my personal experience the answer is clearly that he has not and never will.

Christ rebuilds our lives

I make all things new (Revelation 21:5).

A divorced Christian man has to start rebuilding his life all over again. This can be quite a challenge, but the Christian man can be certain of God's purposes for him.

* What new direction does God have for your life? Are you asking him and talking this over with friends? No matter what has happened, God continues to work out his plan in your life. Abraham's life might help here—read of his mistakes in Egypt, and of God's continuing friendship and purposes (Genesis 12 and 13).

* What skills and talents can you offer him now, that you couldn't offer him before? Your experience will have changed you considerably and God can use that change.

* Are there other divorced men that you can offer friendship to now?

* In what ways are you making friends socially, so that you can build bridges for Christ?

There are many other possibilities now open to you, but it's up to you to make the positive effort to take them. Will you?

Christ gives you family

> The group of believers was one in mind and heart (Acts 4:32).

The divorced man has the family of his local fellowship to support and help him. The believers provide spiritual strength and practical support. The Christian man can find people here to help him with the practical jobs that he can't manage himself. He can also enjoy female company in a controlled setting, and give and receive from God.

Does your local fellowship provide you with this kind of support? If it doesn't, then you must lovingly make other members aware of your needs. If you're a married member of the fellowship, are you aware of the needs of divorced men in your church? Do you offer support, and your home to them?

I want to finish this section with three comments on divorce:

Some divorces seem necessary. I don't condone divorce, but over the years I have seen some marriages end and this has been a blessing to both parties. When physical or mental abuse gets beyond endurance, or when children are being mistreated, then divorce seems the only option.

Women can help. Divorced men have great needs, but unlike divorced women, won't come looking for help. Married women with a stable marriage can be of the greatest assistance, both practically and spiritually. It is important that they remain aware of the risks involved, and if they can offer the support of their home, then these risks are minimized. But divorced men do need female support.

Divorce is not the end of the world. God is able to be

creative in any situation, and he can turn all things to good if we give him the chance. Are you going to give him this opportunity?

THE WIDOWER

Another man who has to come to terms with singleness is the widower. As with divorce, the widower has a whole grief process to go through, but unlike the divorced man, his situation is not interpreted as one of failure, or in any way unnatural.

Like the divorced man, he has to come to terms with being without many things that he has previously known. Many of us will enter this state, although statistically, we are more likely to die before our wives, or else remarry after they have died. Being a widower is a challenge for all men, Christian or otherwise. There are certain experiences that come to all widowers which I want to outline before looking at the Christian perspective. If you have friends who are widowers, or members of your church fellowships, make a special point of applying what you read to them.

Bereavement

He has the whole process of bereavement ahead of him—the shock, the pain and bewilderment, the adjusting to a new situation, and finding a meaning in life—and he has to do this without his lifelong companion. Of course, he has to do it 'like a man', with as few tears as possible, and an apparent ability to cope which will impress his friends—although hopefully not the more discerning ones.

Rebuilding his life

A widower feels that the centre of his life has been taken away. For years—maybe many years—he has merged his life with another, and now he's on his own. It's a difficult process of readjustment, and it can be a very lonely one.

Becoming a homemaker

All the jobs that were once shared are now his to do. He has to become cook, housemaid and decorator. In fact, he becomes the homemaker and men are not generally equipped for this task. We can learn it, but it's not easy.

Loneliness

A widower knows loneliness, and unlike widows he doesn't find it easy to make friends—friends who will really help him. There are many groups for widows, but very few for widowers, and anyway men don't necessarily like going to groups. This loneliness is intensified when he sees other couples, and then has to come back to his empty house. Holidays are a problem, not just because there isn't anyone to go with, but because wherever he goes his memories will go with him.

The children

If a widower is young, then he may have the responsibility of caring for children—young or teenage. To be Mother and Father is a tough job. Many women have to face this as well, but they seem better equipped than men to handle it.

Infirmity

If a widower is older, then he has to face the possibility

of illness and incapacity. It's hard for a man to face incapacity, and facing it alone is a particularly heavy burden.

Sexuality

A widower is a man, and has to come to terms with his sexual nature. He has to do this in a world which is adapted for married people, and where his desire for female company can so easily be misunderstood.

Money worries and a secure home

This is quite a problem for a man faced with living alone on one income—or a limited one. Even those men with no apparent money worries face an uncertain future. As one man said: 'Even with money in your pocket, you have to be motivated to go on living.'

The Christian widower has some very encouraging resources to help and direct him. If ever faith provides a man with a firm foundation, it's at this moment in his life.

The Christian widower

Death is not our enemy

> Death is destroyed; victory is complete! (1 Corinthians 15:54).

Christian men have a means of understanding and coming to terms with death. The very heart of our faith is that Jesus has overcome death with all its pain, grief and fear. We don't have to be defeatist or fatalistic. Death is a creative experience, opening up for us new closeness to God.

If we have this certainty in our own heart, then we can face the death of our wife more realistically. When King David's child was at the point of death, he prayed with great intensity. But when the child finally died, he adopted a realistic attitude:

> While the child was still alive, I fasted and wept. I thought, 'Who knows? The Lord may be gracious to me and let the child live.' But now that he is dead, why should I fast? Can I bring him back again? I will go to him, but he will not return to me (2 Samuel 12:22, NIV).

I have shared the grief of many hundreds of people in my years as a pastor. I know how hard it is to face the future without a beloved wife and partner. But I have noticed again and again that the Christian men are able to get strength from their love of Christ, and from their awareness of his power over death. They are able, in time, to share David's attitude.

If you love Christ and have lost your wife, let the certainty of Christ's total victory over death strengthen you today. If you know men who have lost their wives, then make a special point of praying for them and asking them if there's any practical way you can help.

A new perspective

> Let us keep our eyes fixed on Jesus (Hebrews 12:2).

A friend of mine said this when he lost his wife, 'After her death, I felt the loss as much as anyone else. But then I realized that my life was a series of empty rooms and I had a choice. I could either fill those rooms with anger and remorse, or I could fill them with Jesus, and this helped me get a new perspective on my life. I had gone with my wife into the valley of death as far as I could go. Then I could go no further, and she went on alone. Slowly, my life has developed a new centre, and I've got a new perspective. I haven't stopped loving my wife, but she isn't the centre of my earthly life any more.'

This new perspective doesn't come quickly or easily, but for the man who has his eyes fixed on Jesus, it must come, because Jesus makes things new. Philip died three years ago, and I'm only just beginning to be able to handle the memories and feel a release and a new purpose coming to that part of my life which has been almost dead since it all happened.

Is a new way of seeing things coming into your life? If it is, then thank God for it, and ask him to give you a chance to share this with other men in the same position as you who do not know Christ.

Handling our emotions

> Cast all your anxiety on him because he cares for you (1 Peter 5:7, NIV).

A widower, like the rest of us, needs to express his inner feelings and emotions. There's no easy answer here, and it's very important to find someone with whom you can share on a personal level. The men of the Bible have experienced and shown all the emotions that you feel—tears, despair, frustration, anger, sorrow and all the rest, so don't be ashamed to share these things with Christ, and with your friend. Sometimes it helps to go to a lonely place and spend time with God. Do you have a lonely place for this purpose?

Our material needs

> My God will meet all your needs according to his glorious

> riches in Christ Jesus (Philippians 4:19, NIV).

The Christian man knows that he can depend on God for all his needs—spiritual, emotional and physical. It's a matter of considerable amazement to non-Christians that God does provide food, furniture and finance to those who trust in him. We don't have to 'wait for something to turn up'. We know that God will provide all our needs. Look back over the years and remember some of the things God has already given you—and thank him for them now. Do you have material needs at this moment? Then bring them all to God right now.

The church family

> The group of believers was one in mind and heart (Acts 4:32).

Belonging to a fellowship of believers should give to the widower the things he needs the most—friendship, support, social time, female company and a sense of continued usefulness and purpose. Does your fellowship provide these things? If it doesn't then you've got a responsibility to help the members see their responsibility to you and others like you.

If you're married, do you make the effort as a fellowship and as individuals to include the widowers in your social groupings rather than waiting to be asked? Can you be accused of keeping them out because you haven't been aware of their needs?

6

A Man Growing Old

I was thirty-eight yesterday, and to celebrate the day we all went out for a walk. On the way we passed a very old man. He was bent over his walking stick, making careful progress over a bumpy pavement. I remember thinking quite clearly, 'You're thirty-eight today, Jim. That could be you in thirty-eight years' time—if you make it that far!'

Unless we die on the way, we will all pass into the state of old age. What is this ageing process, and how does a Christian man see it compared to a non-Christian man? To answer this question, we need first to understand some of the issues of growing old.

Ageing is not an experience that comes to us at some arbitrary point in our lives. We used to use the expression 'old age pensioner' a lot, but I notice that this is being replaced more appropriately with the title 'senior citizen'. 'Old age pensioner' suggests that once we have retired from paid work, we pass into that phase of our lives known as 'ageing'. But we begin to age from the cradle, and the process of getting old soon becomes apparent. When I was twenty-five, I used to run a summer camp for young people, and I would want to do all the sporting activities.

At thirty, I began to discover that the young people were getting a bit faster than me. At thirty-five, I retired from the sports, deciding to leave all that sort of thing to the young leaders. It was either this, or get run off my feet! Throughout our middle years, we can become more aware of the ageing process. Our thinking is not as flexible as it used to be; we're much more sure that our way is right and that others are wrong; physically we may notice weaknesses; annoying little things happen to our bodies; we can't recover quite as quickly from illness, and it takes longer to recover from long, tiring journeys.

Perhaps it's better to see our lives as a gradual ageing process, rather than something that happens to us at a clearly defined moment. At least this way we're better prepared. However, there does come a period of time when we are aware that we are old, and others are aware of it as well. We could define such a period as:

* The awareness that we have limited health, mobility and flexibility of thought.
* The ending of paid work, with major adjustments in lifestyle, income, friendships and purpose.
* The awareness that death cannot be far away—a fact emphasized by the illness and death of lifetime friends.
* The world as we know it is fading away, and other men with other ideas are leading.
* Dependence on other people becomes more a part of our lives, especially with the onset of incapacity.

There are of course satisfactions in old age, which can

compensate for the other inconveniences. For example:

* There's the satisfied past, and the sense of a job well done, a life well spent.
* Time to develop new skills and abilities.
* Time for family and friends.
* Time to relax and think.

Growing old necessitates living creatively with these benefits and difficulties. All men—Christian and non-Christian—have to sort their thinking and attitudes out. What is special about the Christian man?

THE CHRISTIAN OLDER MAN

God's timeless framework

> When Abram was seventy-five years old, he started out from Haran, as the Lord had told him (Genesis 12:4).

Seventy-five must be considered as at least the beginning of old age in any culture. Yet at that age, Abraham began his major work for God—a work which would take him well beyond his hundredth year. Age doesn't seem to have a lot of relevance to God. Young and old alike are called into his service, and inexperience or incapacity do not seem to affect his willingness to use us. If you are an older person, you can be secure in the knowledge that your age is no hindrance to God. What do you think he might be calling you to do for him today, in whatever situation you find yourself?

Never worthless to God

> For only a penny you can buy two sparrows, yet not one sparrow falls to the ground without your Father's consent. As for you, even the hairs of your head have all been counted. So do not be afraid; you are worth much more than many sparrows! (Matthew 10:29–31).

Older men often feel useless and very vulnerable. But these feelings find no echo in the heart of God. Each one of us is of unique value to him, precious and special. If a dead bird has a place in his heart, then perhaps we can catch a glimpse of how important we are to him. Have you lost sight of this truth under the pressure of ageing? We are useful to him, valued servants with much experience of his workings to use for our own benefit, and to share with others who are less experienced in his service. Do you accept this position of elder statesmen, who can, with humility and gentleness, help those younger than you? Or have you become too wrapped up in your own problems to see this privilege? We are protected by him in a violent world that has little respect for age and infirmity. Are you leaning on his protection daily?

Suffering can be understood

> He was humble and walked the path of obedience all the way to death—his death on the cross (Philippians 2:8).

A Christian man has a philosophy that can cope with suffering, weakness and pain. He cannot avoid it, nor does he have all the answers. But he does understand that ultimately all things are in the hands of God—a God who understands suffering and pain, because he himself went through so much. The physical sufferings of Christ often speak clearly to non-Christian men, and these same sufferings can be a strength to us as we suffer pain. All Christ's masculinity was stripped away in his suffering and death—and this is one of the things we fear, isn't it? But Christ was able to cope, because he knew that this was the Father's will.

Do you lean on Christ as you suffer physical pain and mental uncertainty? It might be worth reading the story of Christ's crucifixion regularly, and trying to picture the event. This will keep your sufferings in context and help you endure to the end.

Death is not the end

> Death is destroyed;
> Victory is complete! (1 Corinthians 15:54).

I'm all for living my life to the full. I want to know Christ *now*, and I can honestly say that Christ has given me this experience of fullness. Yet it is at the point of death that Christian men have the biggest advantage over the world. We know that Jesus has destroyed death, and that as we die, we pass into his presence for ever. The older we get, the more we need this assurance, because we know that death must be nearer to us. Can you face death with this quiet assurance? If you are a surrendered Christian man, and you've got doubts, then spend a few minutes thinking about the love that God has for you, read these verses, and ask for God's assurance.

> I am telling you the truth: he who believes has eternal life (John 6:47).

> I am the resurrection and the life. Whoever believes in me will live, even though he dies; and whoever lives and believes in me will never die (John 11:25).

If you're not a Christian man, then you cannot have any assurance in the face of death without Christ. Is it time to surrender?

You have a family

The church family should be the place where older Christian men can give and receive. The fellowship should be able to alleviate isolation and loneliness, help in practical ways, and give every encouragement to use the experience and wisdom of the years. At the same time, older men can give their time and services to the work of God through the fellowship. Do you still give your time and attention to your local fellowship? Perhaps you can't get to the Sunday services as often as you would like to, but that's only a part of church life. There are many ways in which you can help and serve—but are you willing to do so?

Do you, as a fellowship, consider the needs of older men? Do you pray for them, and visit regularly to pray and share with them? Do you provide a tape or video service? Do you involve them in decision-making? In other words, do you include them *in*, rather than *out?* Are you inadvertently overlooking one of your greatest resources?

If you are married to an older Christian man, then you have a vital part to play in helping your husband to give his very best to Christ.

* He's still the head of the home, and your loving submission to him will do much to help him realize his continued worth to God. Will you continue in this position, especially if illness and infirmity mean that you have to do more for him than ever before? This is a big thing to ask, but it's so easy for a woman to take over under these circumstances, and this only undermines the older Christian husband.

* He needs encouragement to stay in active service within the fellowship. When younger men come along, it's easy for him to feel threatened and want to pull out. Your encouragement will make a very big difference.

* He needs criticism. It's so easy for older men to believe that they are always right! Your loving and creative criticism will help him recognize that others have a point of view which needs listening to and respecting. This will prevent him becoming isolated in the fellowship.

* He needs an area of service. Sometimes men don't see what they can do for God. You can be on the lookout for things that he can do—prayer, visiting, encouraging others. Will you do this for your husband?

* He needs Christian male company. You are in a position to encourage him to go to men's events, go out with his friends and so on. Often your own judgement with words such as, 'Go out with them, Jim. It will do you good,' will make all the difference.

7

The Christian Man

As I've prepared and written this book, and *Manhunt* before it, certain key thoughts about a Christian man have impressed themselves on me, and I want to end by looking at them, and the challenge that they present to us.

A man has great weaknesses

There's no doubt about it—men have great weaknesses in their characters. Even though we like to appear strong, underneath we are very weak. Our outward appearance of strength only makes it more difficult for us to deal with our weaknesses. We're denied the right to cry or get out of control, we are not encouraged to speak of love, need and care. Women need tenderness, and so do we, but the image prevents us giving or receiving it.

The Christian man can accept this about himself because he has surrendered to a stronger man than himself, and that stronger man is able to turn these very weaknesses to his advantage. One of the most amazing verses in the Bible for a man is this one: 'When I am weak, then I am strong' (2 Corinthians 12:10).

It seems so back-to-front, yet this is the point at which God is most able to work through us. Some of the best things I have ever accomplished in God's service have been while I've felt unwell. Philip's death completely broke my spirit, and it's still broken, yet after he had died, I noticed that there was a difference in my preaching, and people seemed to listen with greater intensity.

The challenge to the Christian man is this: will you accept your own weakness? Will you let others see your weakness, so that they can get close to the source of your strength? Will you let God lower you in your own estimation, so that others can see him more clearly in you?

There is a unique place for man in God's plan

The masculine approach to life and its challenges is very different from the feminine one. It isn't better or worse, but it is different because God has made it that way. He made us male and female, not unisex, and that's the way he wants things to work—with a male and a female approach to things.

When we occupy this position, with all its responsibilities, we're not male chauvinists trying to usurp a role given to women. We're simply being obedient to God's plan and purpose for his creation. As I work out my male role in my home, my work, my social life and my church alongside the women, I know that God's plans will mature. Any abdication from my male position will be seen by him as disobedience.

The challenge to Christian men is to believe in this unique calling, and to look to God for the fulfilling of it. This might involve a lot of rethinking. Perhaps you have had a chauvinist attitude in some things and that has to go. Maybe you have been disobedient in some ways and this has to change.

A Christian man has great potential

There is a great potential for God's work locked up in the hearts and lives of the Christian men of the world. The Christian women have been out on their own for long enough. It's time for the Christian men to get serious and come out to join them.

I'm not going to outline all the possibilities open to a Christian man—you will have encountered many of them in these pages. The question and challenge is this: will you start praying to God, asking him to show you what you as a man in his service can do for him? Imagine what a prayer storm would hit the gates of heaven if hundreds of thousands of Christian men all over the world started praying, 'God, what can we do as Christian men in your service? Everything we have is at your disposal.'

God would have a lot on his hands, or rather in his hands, but if he is able to feed five thousand with a few loaves, imagine what he is able to do with his hands full!

A Christian man needs his wife

The more I read the Bible and examine God's ways for me, the more I become aware of how much I need my wife to help me appreciate and fulfil my calling. By being the good and submissive wife, she allows me room to develop my servant headship, and my understanding of myself. How feminists see this as a subservient role I find difficult to understand. I know that I can only be the man God intended me to be, if Mary will be the woman God intended her to be, and the wife he planned for her to be. I count it a privilege to be her servant husband.

The challenge is clear—will you accept your servant headship position? If you won't, then you'll have less trouble with the world, but your marriage will never be fulfilled in God's sight, and your children will perpetuate your disobedience. If you will, the benefits are truly wonderful for all concerned.

Non-Christian men need Christian men

Yesterday we all went out shopping. We couldn't get the pram into one shop, so I waited outside while the family went in. I watched the crowds passing by and there were many men. They all looked so confident and sure of themselves, and I got quite depressed. How would I ever be able to help these men find Christ for themselves? If I went up to them there and then to speak about my faith, they would probably ignore me, laugh at me, or push me away.

But I know that each one of these men belongs to a network of people elsewhere—family, friends, work colleagues and social acquaintances. Suppose that somewhere in that network there was a man living out his life for Christ to the full and showing the Christian difference in every way. Then it does become possible for these men in the street, with whom I have no contact, to find out about Christ and to surrender to him for themselves.

It seems to me to be of the highest importance that every Christian man is living out his Christian life to the full wherever he lives or works. This is of more importance to the total work of the church than any mission, crusade or social programme. If non-Christian men do not see Christ making the difference in us, they won't have much time for speakers, evangelists or social activities.

My men in the street needed that Christian man in their network—needed him more than they could ever know.

Are you their man?

Manhunt

by Jim Smith

A new enthusiasm fills many churches today. Numbers are growing; worship is becoming a richer experience; 'evangelism' is a word on everyone's lips.

But where are the men?

Jim Smith writes from a sense of urgency and expectancy. In this book he shows how a church can become far more relevant and attractive to men—husbands, single men, teenagers, workers, unemployed. Starting from a review of how Jesus himself worked, he goes on to spell out how the church can reach men on a much larger scale. Only then will this nation feel the impact of the gospel in a radical and dynamic way.

Jim Smith is an evangelist with the Church Pastoral Aid Society. He was chairman for counselling and follow-up for Mission England in the north-east, and was involved in youth training and outreach.

Foolish to be Wise

by Roy Peacock

As a scientist, Roy Peacock had a mind trained for meticulous observation. His understanding of the world seemed watertight.

But his growing cynicism about the world of the supernatural did not go unchallenged. Through a series of meetings with Christians of simple but vital faith, the foundations of his thinking and way of life were to be radically shaken.

The events that followed are related here in a way that is both lucid and gripping. Through it all we see that it is not necessary to jettison a passion for truth in order to encounter the God of the Bible, but that false prejudices must die if we are to walk by faith and know God's presence in our lives today.

PROFESSOR ROY PEACOCK has been on the faculty of two postgraduate universities and is the author of many scientific papers. He has been at the forefront of research in aeronautical engineering, and has lectured in many countries by government invitation.

Kingsway Publications

For the Love of Mike

by Sherwood Eliot Wirt

Mike MacIntosh was a 'free spirit' of the sixties, a child of the peace movement. But freedom came to mean little more than drifting like a wandering star through a nightmare world of emptiness and pain. Hitch-hiking, job-switching and living rough, he crashed through two broken marriages, drug-induced hallucinations and confinement to a mental ward, before he was finally brought to the end of himself.

It was then that Mike made a discovery that was to lead to complete healing and the restoration of his first marriage. With a new-found love for Jesus Christ, and a desire to reach out to others in need, Mike began a ministry that has since taken the good news of Christ's love to thousands.

'A message of hope to those whose lives have been marred and twisted by the underside of modern culture.' Billy Graham

k

Kingsway Publications